Reclaiming Authenticity

A Psycho-Spiritual Process of
Transformation and Transcendence

James A. Houck Jr., PhD

WESTBOW°
PRESS
A DIVISION OF THOMAS NELSON
& ZONDERVAN

WestBow Press books may be ordered through booksellers or by contacting:

WestBow Press
A Division of Thomas Nelson & Zondervan
1663 Liberty Drive
Bloomington, IN 47403
www.westbowpress.com
1 (866) 928-1240

ISBN: 978-1-4908-3952-3 (sc)

Library of Congress Control Number: 2014910001

Printed in the United States of America.

WestBow Press rev. date: 6/18/2014

DEDICATION

*Dedicated to all who have the courage to
discover who they are, whose they are, and
reclaim their authenticity in an inauthentic world.*

CONTENTS

INTRODUCTION

The call to live a more authentic life is becoming increasingly poignant these days. It seems that everywhere we turn; genuineness and authenticity are rare characteristics among people who are searching for palpable substance in relationships. Nowadays, society is rapidly conditioning generations to question the motives and desires of others like never before. For example, personal image is at an all-time fever pitch as one reality show after another presents us with anything but reality. Daily we are being sold the message to be the most socially acceptable persona that money can buy. In fact, it seems as though the more drama and tears, the better the front-page story. Who can out-shock who? Who can accumulate more toys and points than anyone else? Who has more guile, more trickery? Who is more cunning either by hook or by crook? Cut-throat politics and religious scandals have saturated the daily news as bewildered people in coffee shops and bars look at each other wondering how much worse can it get?

Instead of taking people at face value, we now are accustomed to ask *"what's the catch?"* Perhaps as a result of a number of humiliating and painful experiences, we avoid any further investing of physical, emotional or spiritual parts of ourselves in relationships. Furthermore, out of our brokenness, we may feel that we just cannot risk being a victim to yet another example of fraud, trickery and/or dishonesty. Past physical, psychological and spiritual wounding has taken too much out of us, leaving us to believe that others simply conspire to take advantage of our vulnerability.

And yet, isn't this the dilemma we face? To strive for genuineness and authenticity in our relationships demands a level of vulnerability from us. In other words, before we can expect and appreciate authenticity from another, we are forced to confront our own inconsistent and inauthentic ways. Author and family psychotherapist Virginia Satir (1916-1988) sums up this sentiment nicely:

> *I want to love you without clutching,*
> *Appreciate you without judging*
> *Join you without invading,*
> *Invite you without demanding,*
> *Leave you without guilt,*
> *Criticize you without blaming,*
> *And help you without insulting.*
> *If I can have the same from you,*
> *Then we can truly meet each other.*

As idealistic as this kind of human interaction sounds, genuineness and authenticity in relationships are tangible, but does indeed require a life-long commitment to self-discovery and honesty about who we are with warts, gifts, phobias, strengths, graces, and all. Unfortunately, this commitment is a price many consider too high to pay and not worth their time. Would it not be easier to be satisfied with the status quo, go with the flow and not question? Of course, that might be the *frequently traveled road*, but let us not deceive ourselves: The inner desire for genuineness and authenticity in relationship with ourselves, others and God is not going away. Moreover, that internal longing to be more authentic and true to ourselves will only get stronger. The question is how much more sleep do we want to keep losing night after night? How many more times are we going to blame others for what we don't have?

The Ancient Wisdom of Mountains

Writing from the perspective of one who loves to hike mountains, I have found there is a striking parallel between our search for authenticity and how the ancient wisdom of mountains, literally and figuratively, give us a glimpse into our desire for psycho-spiritual transformation. Quite simply, mountains have much to teach us. Every year, every season, from rainfall to snowfall, generation to generation, mountains remain the stable giants in our landscape. Since the beginning of time, people have had a fascination with mountains spending their lives and small fortunes climbing the highest mountains in the world. Perhaps this appeal to climb comes from our attraction to a mountain's immensity and majesty or to satisfy the sense of a higher calling in our lives. At any rate, people today are being inwardly led to withdraw from society and live in these mountains, develop their spiritual abilities, and connect with the yearning that led spiritual leaders to seek God on the mountain top.

Ancient China recorded five sacred directional mountains that stretch across its country in which the sages dwelled and emperors made life-long pilgrimages to seek the blessings of heaven (Naquin, 1992). These include:

- *Eastern Mountain (Tai Shan), Shandong providence*
- *Northern Great Mountain (Heng Shan Bei), Shanxi providence*
- *Western Great Mountain (Hua Shan), Shanxi providence*
- *Southern Great Mountain (Shan Nan), Hunan Providence*
- *Central Mountain (Song Shan), Henan providence*

These mountains, or five peaks (wu-yueh), are central to the religion of Taoism, i.e., living in harmony with the way or path. They were considered powerful spiritual locations that paralleled the cardinal directions, and were believed to be pillars that separated heaven from earth. According to ancient Chinese cosmology, the realm of heaven covered the realm of earth and from this belief came the idea that heaven could fall down if not supported. Thus, the different energies of these mountains influenced the spiritual traditions that grew on each of them, as the mountains themselves were believed to house spiritual energies.

In another example, Croagh Patrick is the most important Catholic pilgrimage destination in Ireland. Following in the footsteps of St. Patrick, who spent 40 days fasting on the mountain in the year 441 AD, nearly one million pilgrims climb to the top every year. Following his fast it is believed that St. Patrick rang a bell so loudly that the sound drove all the evil spirits and snakes out of Ireland. For most people then the pilgrimage to the top of the sacred mountain is an act of penance, often remembering St. Patrick's devotion, by reaching the summit on their knees or walking barefoot.

Tewa Native American mystic, ceremonial dancer, artist, and writer, Joseph Rael (Beautiful Painted Arrow, 1993) emphasizes how mountains metaphorically refer to the human heart:

> *The traditional form of a vision quest was to reach the top of a mountain. Going to the top of a mountain or any high place, has the quality, symbolically, of going to the heart or center of vibration, where we search not just for ordinary awareness, but for the highest possibility in conscious awareness. The mountain top is in the environment for the highest potential because the vibration of light there is of very high quality. It is on top of a vision quest mountain where heart and mind are bonded together* (Being and Vibration, pg. 109).

Indeed it appears that people from various cultures, religions and languages recognize a psycho-spiritual connection to at least one of hundreds of mountains throughout the world. In fact, depending if you have a favorite mountain and if you have ever climbed a mountain top and looked over a valley or at the sight, you know how this has changed you. Indeed the view can be breathtaking! Looking in the six directions of above, below, north, south, east and west, one can really grasp the proportion of how small we are in comparison to the vast world. Perhaps it is this realization that we are drawn to mountains because we are stirred to reconnect with our hearts. Throughout history many battles have been fought on or close to mountains, perhaps as a means of reflecting the heart's inner struggle. Perhaps we climb mountains to get away from a disconnected world and conditional relationships, to reconnect with ourselves and God. Painter, author, art educator and therapist Peter London (2003) notes how external landscapes have a lot to teach us about our internal landscapes:

> *Each of the great forms that Earth takes...mountains and hills and plains and valleys and meadows and steppes and swamps, and marshes and deserts and forests and jungles and savannahs and beaches and islands—each of these geographies we transmute to geobiographies of our own personal journey across time and circumstance...the finite summit of the mountain peak, the river's final arrival to the sea, the clearing in the depths of the woods, serve as exemplars and as metaphors for the often steep and uncertain and perilous journey that is our life.*

And yet, when we gaze at or climb mountains we may not realize the physical, psychological and spiritual interdependence we have with mountains for our survival and well-being. For example, people and wildlife depend upon mountains for its agricultural and forest benefits, as well as for their source of water and nutrients. We have come to depend on their minerals (such as coal, iron ore, shale, methane, copper, gold, clay, silver, nickel, chromium, etc.) for our everyday use. Mountains also provide a safe habitat and conservation for wildlife, as well as affect climate conditions, such as blocking much of the wind and moisture on the windward side of them. Lastly, mountains are also known for their aesthetic beauty and recreational opportunities as avid hikers and national park enthusiasts visit them year after year.

Still, there is a lot of talk these days about reducing our carbon footprints from eliminating greenhouse gases and industrial emissions, and the effects of mining, to the global warming debate and conservation. Yet, what I do not hear included in this conversation is how the damaging effects our carbon footprints clearly mimic the damaging effects our "interpersonal footprints" have on one another. Today, it is often considered the norm, if not the expectation, that people will walk all over one another; to lie, cheat and steal, and then expect that these actions will have no psychological or spiritual consequences. If we assume this we are gravely mistaken. As evidenced from our attitudes and actions we have not learned from previous generations' discoveries and mistakes. We clearly do not possess the ancient wisdom that comes from recognizing those lessons of respect, dignity, value and gratitude passed on to us in the created order of things. To put it another way, it ought to be glaringly obvious that the way we treat our environmental resources and animals is a direct reflection of our attitudes and behaviors toward each other. In fact, despite all our searching for psycho-spiritual wholeness, we do not possess such wisdom because we do not understand how we are spiritually and emotionally fragmented. However,

9

it is from this understanding that we recognize the opportunity that is before us to heal this relationship to ourselves, others and the land.

The Land Remembers

For those who seek a heightened psycho-spiritual awareness, mountains also have a lot to teach us about *inter*personal (with God and others) and *intra*personal (with ourselves) relationships. As previously mentioned, standing at their base, mountains remind us just how small we are in comparison. As we hike or climb, we are struck by the beauty and splendor of life that surrounds us. Upon reaching the summit, many people sense a stronger connection to themselves and to God, as well as perceive a greater perspective of the world below. In those moments we have a greater awakening of how our uniqueness has been gifted by God, as well as our growing edges and vulnerable areas we have yet to surrender to God. In this sense, we are overcome with a sense of gratitude and understanding. Even though we may not know what we might discover about ourselves, people continue to seek God with the help of mountains. Moreover, whatever we experience can be a powerful psycho-spiritual transformation that leaves us unlike we were before. Yet herein lies the irony of humanity: History has demonstrated how some people are only drawn to mountains to extract their minerals but are not drawn to people. In other words, people will often sell their souls for all the natural resources they can procure, while at the same time, throwing away the most important resource of all, namely relationships established by a loving Creator's hand.

This psycho-spiritual *disconnection* is something the land does not forget. The land indeed remembers. Souls and souls have trekked the land for countless generations. The air they breathed is the same air we breathe. The same sources of water from which they drank we drink. The same mountains they have climbed for psycho-spiritual renewal we climb today. These literal and spiritual paths have been blazed for us to follow and our imprint does not go unnoticed. As we walk in the footprints of our ancestors and relations, as a great cloud of witnesses (Hebrews 12:1), they carefully observe our attitudes and actions. Yes, the land remembers. . .through the countless violence and aggression throughout history in which the stain is communicated. Even the blood of those who have laid slain cry out from the land (Genesis 4:10), which is imprinted with the horrors of genocide and desolation. We may attempt to forget about these tragedies, as the so-called history books are written from a softer perspective that romanticizes the harsh reminders of the depraved human interaction. However, the echoes of pain and suffering tell us that their stories need to be heard and told:

> *I listen to the screams of the wounded and dying carried on the wind across the prairie. Blood spilled in the ground. We forget about these things, but the trees...they remember, the rocks...they remember, and the earth...it remembers. They remember when we forget. The story is forever imprinted, imprinted on this land. If we listen they will guide us, give us visions,*

*tell us stories. Past, present and future all touch one
another. Time does not exist. For spirits, time does not
exist. Can you hear them? Can you hear their cries?*
Imprint: 2007, Linn Productions

By inviting us to understand how mountains teach us
about authenticity, we certainly are called to heal from our
psycho-spiritual wounds, and to reclaim our connectedness to
all living things. We not only discover who we are in relation
to all of creation, but we also understand that we are stewards,
entrusted with the care of the world that provides for us. A
vital aspect of this connection is to develop ways to reconnect
those fragmented areas of our lives that have been separated
by loss, pain, or trauma. After careful introspection of our
woundedness, we may realize that we have intentionally, or
unintentionally, given away parts of ourselves as a means of
survival. Native American Chippewa activist Sun Bear (1989)
refers to this kind of behavior as giving away our personal
power, leaving us with little to no precious emotional energy
to live genuinely. Today, mental health professionals refer to
this giving away of ourselves as "dissociation." Dissociation
occurs whenever we emotionally or physically detach or
separate ourselves in situations (reality) that have become
overwhelming or life-threatening. Examples range from simply
daydreaming to relieve stress or boredom, to more severe cases
of amnesia which the brain protects us from further traumatic
damage, abuse and conflict. In severe cases, the diagnosis of
dissociative identity disorder is given when a person's situation

is so emotionally and/or physically overwhelming that there is a fragmentation of a his/her identity and perceived reality. Consequently, an alternative identity emerges to habitually further shield or protect the wounded, vulnerable self.

In talking to others who have climbed mountains and listened to its ancient wisdom, some people find their experience similar to different parts of a symphony. For example, there is a point in a symphony where the music begins softly then swells to a heart-beating crescendo. The melody carries us along, till we find ourselves at the very height of its music when the sound of cymbals crash and the timpani thunders a vibration in our hearts and throats. We feel our spirits lifted, almost as if as though we have been taken to a higher, better place, outside of ourselves. Magically transformed, it is within this atmosphere of sound where we want to stay because the feelings are euphoric. Perhaps it is within this moment of sound we are able to transcend something in ourselves that we have been unable to do by other means. However, just as quickly as there is a crescendo, there is a descent, bringing our feet back down to earth; back down to the everyday sounds of traffic, conversations and machines. Still, we tell ourselves we have been on a great journey which we want to retain for as long as possible. That music carries us as we leave the concert hall, auditorium or theatre, and it is this distant memory of music we try to get back to. And just as we have to leave the concert hall, we too have to come down from the mountain and live out in relationships what we have encountered. If we have not invested time and authenticity in these relationships, we may find ourselves as emotionally empty and spiritually emaciated as the land itself that has been stripped of its resources.

Sooner or later we have to return to our daily routines and discover new ways to live our psycho-spiritual transformative experiences. In as much as we may have experienced an exhilarating psycho-spiritual transformation, the irony is that these life-changing moments are not necessarily for ourselves. Indeed, just as strong as the experience of psycho-spiritual transformation is, we are then called to transcend these "mountain-top" experiences by getting beyond our self-serving attitudes, co-dependent behaviors, and embrace our mutually-shared connection to one another. In other words, shifting our focus from what do we get out of this to

- *How do we keep it, to how are we gifted to serve others?*
- *How can we live a life of authenticity that is life-giving to the emotional, physical and spiritual well-being of ourselves and others?*
- *Where does this transformation first take place in us?*
- *Exactly what is transformed?*
- *Are there certain times in our lives when we are more "ripe" for transformation or do we just happen to be in the right place at the right time?*
- *Are we simply responding to God's call, stirring our hearts and nudging us along?*

Regardless of the questions, being aware of God's Spirit in our lives always requires a response from us; an act of faith.

Remember, ignoring God and an indecisiveness to take the initial steps of self-discovery is also a response. Yes, psycho-spiritual transformation is initiated by God, but it also is an intentional, daily effort on our behalf; it is not a passive phenomenon. It requires an active participation or work on our part. Transformation places us on a path, a journey to follow and embrace all of what God has in store for us. Yet, transformation also compels us to *transcend* ourselves and our surroundings in order to fan the flames of the internal spiritual fire that has been sparked in us. From the Christian perspective, psycho-spiritual transformation results in a life of service to others following the example of how Jesus Christ served healed and redeemed humanity.

As romantic as being on this psycho-spiritual journey sounds, we will be faced with dangerous obstacles that block our way from the social context in which we live. Moreover, not everyone will accept our spiritual journey with open arms. Not everyone we encounter, or attempt to serve, understands or trusts our motives. We are social beings and must contend with cultural norms, rituals and expectations. When these types of reactions occur let us not take society's response personally or discourage us from future efforts. The truth is that there will be times when our spiritual journey takes us beyond social convention. It has to. When we and others recognize this change we are most fortunate. In fact, people who knew us before our transformation may dismiss us, believing that our new attitude is a phase we are going through. Please keep in mind that many are still living with a skeptical *what's the catch?* They may be simply waiting for us to "get over it" and return to the way we used to be. Admittedly, I believe they are in for a long wait. Yet, in response do we ignore the stirrings of our hearts and simply turn our backs on society, or do we understand that what has been transformed in us, compels us to reengage society to heal the suffering of others? Undeniably, once we have been transformed, we never look at life and others the same as we did before, because now we are looking at the world with our awakened soul, and discern every experience through the lens of heaven's perspective. As a result, all things in our lives undergo a transformation; even work becomes a sense of worshipful service (Rael, 1993).

Within every person's journey to seek God, there is a call to on-going authenticity. In other words, to come as we are, no hidden agendas (like we can hide that from God!), no false pretenses; just simply who we are. God has always responded to seekers who worship him with hearts that are truthful and spirits that are broken and longing for His presence! The act of worship flows naturally out of the heartfelt, spiritual desire to know God and dwell in that holy presence. And it is desire that compels us to be genuine in our relationships with others. Indeed, worship at its essence is the response of a heart that is earnestly striving and crying out after the heart of God. Worship flows out of the deep, wrenching, hunger and thirst desire to know God. Not only to know Him but to dwell in Him – to dwell in His presence!

Indeed, our transformation ultimately encourages us to "recognize our capacity for relatedness" (Delio, 2009). For the purpose of this book, then, I am defining "psycho-spiritual transformation" as the *on-going process by which God's character saturates a person in his/her thoughts, behaviors, and styles of relating with ourselves, others and God.* Such transformation is not limited to either the mind or spirit, but instead encapsulates both. Quoting the Dalai Lama, Fr. Richard Rohr (Founding Director of the Center for Action and Contemplation in Albuquerque, New Mexico) states that "*a change of heart is always a change of mind.*" Both faculties must undergo transformation for it to take root and bear fruit in our lives.

THE ASCENSION

A Desire for the Sacred

O God, you are my God, earnestly I seek you; my
soul thirsts for you, my body longs for you, in a dry
and weary land where there is no water. I have seen
you in the sanctuary and beheld your power and
your glory.

Psalm 63:1-2

Mato Paha, or Bear Butte (as it resembles a bear sleeping on its side) is a 4,426-foot mountain, and is revered by the Lakota, Dakota, Nakota, Cheyenne and Arapahoe in the Black Hills of South Dakota as sacred ground. This land is widely believed to be the place where the God of Creation communicates with His people through vision and prayer. Over the centuries, many Native American tribes have traveled to Bear Butte to perform annual prayer ceremonies. Today, this sacred site draws native and non-native people to make annual pilgrimages for spiritual renewal and sustenance. I too have participated in this journey and find a great spiritual connection to the land. Native chiefs such as Red Cloud, Crazy Horse, and Sitting Bull all camped, prayed, and performed ceremonies at Bear Butte during their lifetimes. Sioux tribes often met at Bear Butte to hold their summer gatherings and council. For example, in June 1871, Crazy Horse returned to Bear Butte for his *Hanblecheyapi,* or a vision quest, and foresaw the upcoming Black Hills War. He later returned to his people with this vision to warn and protect them. In 1857, several tribes comprised of Teton, Miniconjou, Oglala, Sans Arc, and Hunkpapa Sioux tribes gathered at the mountain to discuss the increasing number of European settlers on their lands. It was on top of this mountain that the Sioux held their *Oyate Kiwsiyaya*, the Great Reunion of the People. Again, Crazy Horse pledged to resist further "white" encroachment into the Black Hills in 1857 (Ross, 2000). After Crazy Horse's death at Fort Robinson Nebraska, legend has it that his followers buried him near Bear Butte.

In addition to these historical accounts, Bear Butte is also considered sacred because of its location near the Black Hills, a land that contains seven Native American sacred elements – land, air, water, rocks, animals, plants, and fire – surrounding the Butte. These elements also correspond with the Lakota seven sacred ceremonies (*inipi,* sweat ceremony; *nagi uhapi,* soul keeping; *wiwanyank wachipi,* sun dance; *hanblecheya,* vision quest; *hunka kagapi,* the making of relatives; *ishnati alowanpi,* making a girl turning into a woman ceremony; and *tapa wakayapi,* throwing the ball (Brown, 1953). But perhaps it is the story of how the Lakota people were gifted with the sacred white buffalo calf pipe that defines not only who they are as a people, but also why they trace their spiritual significance to the Black Hills.

The Story of the White Buffalo Calf Woman

One summer so long ago that nobody knows how long, the Oceti Shakowin, the seven sacred council fires of the Lakota Oyate, the nation, came together and camped. The sun shone all the time, but there was no game and the people were starving.

Every day they sent scouts to look for game, but the scouts found nothing. Among the bands assembled were the Itazipcho, the Without Bows, who had their own camp circle under their chief, Standing Hollow Horn. Early one morning the chief sent two of his young men to hunt for game. They went on foot, because at that time the Sioux didn't yet have horses. They searched everywhere but could find nothing. Seeing a high hill, they decided to climb it in order to look over the whole country. Halfway up, they saw something coming toward them from far off, but the figure was floating instead of walking. From this they knew that the person was waken, or holy.

At first they could make out only a small moving speck and had to squint to see that it was a human form. But as it came nearer, they realized that it was a beautiful young woman, more beautiful than any they had ever seen, with two round, red dots of face paint on her cheeks. She wore a wonderful white buckskin outfit, tanned until it shone a long way in the sun. It was embroidered with sacred and marvelous designs of porcupine quill, in radiant colors no ordinary woman could have made. This wakan stranger was Ptesan Wi, White Buffalo Woman. In her hands she carried a large bundle and a fan of sage leaves. She wore her blue black hair loose except for a strand at the left side, which was tied up with buffalo fur. Her eyes shone dark and sparkling, with great power in them.

The two young men looked at her openmouthed. One was overawed, but the other desired her body and stretched his hand out to touch her. This woman was lila waken, very sacred, and could not be treated with disrespect. Lightning instantly struck the brash young man and burned him up, so that only a small heap of blackened bones was left. Or as some say that he was suddenly covered by a cloud, and within it he was eaten up by snakes that left only his skeleton, just as a man can be eaten up by lust. To the other scout who had behaved rightly, the White Buffalo Woman said: "Good things I am bringing, something holy to your nation. A message I carry for your people from the buffalo nation. Go back to the camp and tell the people to prepare for my arrival. Tell your chief to put up a medicine lodge with twenty four poles. Let it be made holy for my coming."

This young hunter returned to the camp. He told the chief, and he told the people, what the sacred woman had commanded. The chief told the eyapaha, the crier, and the crier went through the camp circle calling: "Someone sacred is coming. A holy woman approaches. Make all things ready for her." So the people put up the big medicine tipi and waited. After four days they saw the White Buffalo Woman approaching, carrying her bundle before her. Her wonderful white buckskin dress shone from afar. The chief, Standing Hollow Horn, invited her to enter the medicine lodge. She went in and circled the interior sun-wise. The chief addressed her respectfully, saying: "Sister, we are glad you have come to instruct us."

She told him what she wanted done. In the center of the tipi they were to put up an owanka wakan, a sacred altar, made of red earth, with a buffalo skull and a three-stick rack for a holy thing she was bringing. They did what she directed, and she traced a design with her finger on the smoothed earth of the altar. She showed them how to do all this, then circled the lodge again sunwise. Halting before the chief, she now opened the bundle. The holy thing it contained was the chanunpa, the sacred pipe. She held it out to the people and let them look at it. She was grasping the stem with her right hand and the bowl with her left, and thus the pipe has been held ever since. Again the chief spoke, saying: "Sister, we are glad. We have had no meat for some time. All we can give you is water." They dipped some wacanga, sweet grass, into a skin bag of water and gave it to her, and to this day the people dip sweet grass or an eagle wing in water and sprinkle it on a person to be purified.

The White Buffalo Woman showed the people how to use the pipe. She filled it with chanshasha, red willow bark tobacco. She walked around the lodge four times after the manner of Anpetu Wi, the great sun. This represented the circle without end, the sacred hoop, the road of life. The woman placed a dry buffalo chip on the fire and lit the pipe with it. This was peta-owihankeshini, the fire without end, the flame to be passed on from generation to generation. She told them that the smoke rising from the bowl was Tunkashila's breath, the living breath of the great Grandfather Mystery. The White Buffalo Woman showed the people the right way to pray, the right words and the right gestures. She taught them how to sing the pipefilling song and how to lift the pipe up to the sky, toward Grandfather, and down toward Grandmother Earth, to Unci, and then to the four directions of the universe.

"With this holy pipe," she said, "you will walk like a living prayer. With your feet resting upon the earth and the pipe

stem reaching into the sky, your body forms a living bridge between the Sacred Beneath and the Sacred Above. Wakan Tanka smiles upon us, because now we are as one: earth, sky, all living things, the two legged, the four legged, the winged ones, the trees, the grasses. Together with the people, they are all related, one family. The pipe holds them all together. Look at this bowl. Its stone represents the buffalo, but also the flesh and blood of the red man. The buffalo represents the universe and the four directions, because he stands on four legs, for the four ages of man. The buffalo was put in the west by Wakan Tanka at the making of the world, to hold back the waters. Every year he loses one hair, and in every one of the four ages he loses a leg. The Sacred Hoop will end when all the hair and legs of the great buffalo are gone, and the water comes back to cover the Earth. The wooden stem of this chanunpa stands for all that grows on the earth. Twelve feathers hanging from where the stem the backbone joins the bowl the skull are from Wanblee Galeshka, the spotted eagle, the very sacred who is the Great Spirit's messenger and the wisest of all cry out to Tunkashila . Look at the bowl: engraved in it are seven circles of various sizes. They stand for the seven ceremonies you will practice with this pipe, and for the Ocheti Shakowin, the seven sacred campfires of our Lakota nation."

The White Buffalo Woman then spoke to the women, telling them that it was the work of their hands and the fruit of their bodies which kept the people alive. "You are from the mother earth," she told them. "What you are doing is as great as what warriors do." And therefore the sacred pipe is also something that binds men and women together in a circle of love. It is the one holy object in the making of which both men and women have a hand. The men carve the bowl and make the stem; the women decorate it with bands of colored porcupine quills. When a man takes a wife, they both hold the pipe at the same time and red cloth is wound around their hands, thus tying them together for life. The White Buffalo Woman had many things for her Lakota sisters in her sacred womb bag; corn, wasna (pemmican), wild turnip. She taught how to make the hearth fire. She filled a buffalo paunch with cold water and dropped a redhot stone into it. "This way you shall cook the corn and the meat," she told them.

The White Buffalo Woman also talked to the children, because they have an understanding beyond their years. She told them that what their fathers and mothers did was for them, that their parents could remember being little once, and that they, the children, would grow up to have little ones of their own. She told them: "You are the coming generation, that's why you are the most important and precious ones. Some day you will hold this pipe and smoke it. Some day you will pray with it." She spoke once more to all the people: "The pipe is alive; it is a red being showing you a red life and a red road. And this is the first ceremony for which you will use the pipe. You will use it to Wakan Tanka, the Great Mystery Spirit. The day a human dies is always a sacred day. The day when the soul is released to the Great Spirit is another. Four women will become sacred on such a day. They will be the ones to cut the sacred tree, the canwakan, for the sun dance."

She told the Lakota that they were the purest among the tribes, and for that reason Tunkashila had bestowed upon them the holy chanunpa. They had been chosen to take care of it for all the Indian people on this turtle continent. She spoke one last time to Standing Hollow Horn, the chief, saying, "Remember: this pipe is very sacred. Respect it and it will take you to the end of the road. The four ages of creation are in me; I am the four ages. I will come to see you in every generation cycle. I shall come back to you."

The sacred woman then took leave of the people, saying: "Toksha ake wacinyanitin ktelo, I shall see you again." The people saw her walking off in the same direction from which she had come, outlined against the red ball of the setting sun. As she went, she stopped and rolled over four times. The first time, she turned into a black buffalo; the second into a brown one; the third into a red one; and finally, the fourth time she rolled over, she turned into a white female buffalo calf. A white buffalo is the most sacred living thing you could ever encounter.

The White Buffalo Woman disappeared over the Horizon. Sometime she might come back. As soon as she had vanished, buffalo in great herds appeared, allowing themselves to be killed so the people might survive. And from that day on, our relations, the buffalo, furnished the people with everything they needed, meat for their food, skins for their clothes and tipis, bones for their many tools (adapted from *Black Elk Speaks,* Brown, 1953).

The Vision of Sweet Medicine

In addition to the Lakota, Cheyenne people also possess a story that explains not only the reputation of Sweet Medicine as a prophet to their people, but also to the fact that Bear Butte holds a place of significant religious and spiritual importance:

A long time ago the people had no laws, no rules of behavior-they hardly knew enough to survive. And they did shameful things out of ignorance, because they didn't understand how to live. There was one man among them who had a natural sense of what was right. He and his wife were good, hard-working people, a family to be proud of. They knew how to feel ashamed, and this feeling kept them from doing wrong. Their only child was a daughter, beautiful and modest, who had reached the age when girls begin to think about husbands and making a family. One night a man's voice spoke to her in a dream. "You are handsome and strong, modest and young. Therefore Sweet Root will visit you." Dismissing it as just a dream, the girl went cheerfully about her chores the next day. On the following night, however, she heard the voice again: "Sweet Root is coming-woman's medicine which makes a mother's milk flow. Sweet Root is coming as a man comes courting." The girl puzzled over the words when she awoke, but in the end shrugged her shoulders. People can't control their dreams, she thought, and the idea of a visit from a medicine root didn't make any sense.

On the third night the dream recurred, and this time it was so real that a figure seemed to be standing beside the buffalo robe she slept on. He was talking to her, telling her: "Sweet Root is coming; he is very near. Soon he will be with you." On the fourth night she heard the same voice and saw the same figure. Disturbed, she told her mother about it the next morning. "There must be something in it," she said. "It's so real and the voice is so much like a man's voice."

"No, it's just a dream," her mother said. "It doesn't mean anything." But from that time on, the girl felt different. Something was stirring, growing within her, and after a few months, her condition became obvious: she was going to have a baby. She told her parents that no man had touched her, and they believed her. But others would not be likely to, and the girl hid her condition. When she felt the birth pangs coming on, she went out into the prairie far from the camp and built herself a brush shelter. Doing everything herself, she gave birth to a baby boy. She dried the baby, wrapped him in soft moss, and left him there in the wickiup, for in her village a baby without a father would be scorned and treated badly. Praying that someone would find him, she went sadly home to her parents.

At about the same time, an old woman was out searching the prairie for wild turnips, which she dug up with an animal's shoulder blade. She heard crying, and following the sound, came to the wickiup. She was overjoyed to find the baby, as she had never had one of her own. All around the brush shelter grew the sweet root which makes a mother's milk flow; so she named the boy Sweet Medicine. She took him home to her shabby tipi even though she had nothing to offer him but love. In the tipi next to the old woman's lived a young mother who was nursing a small child, and she agreed to nurse Sweet Medicine also. He grew faster and learned faster than ordinary children and was weaned in no time. When he was only ten years old, he had already grown-up wisdom and hunting skill far in advance of his age. But because he had no family and lived at the edge of the camp in a poor tipi, no one paid any attention to Sweet Medicine's exceptional powers.

That year there was a drought, very little game, and much hunger in the village. "Grandmother," he told her, "find me an old buffalo hide- any dried out, chewed up scrap with holes in it will do." The woman searched among the refuse piles and found a wrinkled, brittle piece that the starving dogs had been chewing on. When she brought it to Sweet Medicine, he told her, "Take this to the stream outside the camp, wash it in the flowing water, make it pliable, scrape it clean." After she had done this Sweet Medicine took a willow wand and bent it into a hoop, which he colored with sacred red earth paint. He cut the buffalo hide into one long string and wove it back and forth over the hoop, making a kind of net with an opening in the center. Then he cut four wild cherry sticks, sharpened them to a point, and hardened them in the hearth fire. The next morning he said: "Grandmother, come with me. We're going to play the hoop-and-stick game." He took the hoop and the cherry-wood sticks and walked into the middle of the camp circle. "Grandmother, roll this hoop for me," he said. She rolled the hoop along the ground and Sweet Medicine hurled his pointed sticks through the center of it, hitting the right spot every time. Soon a lot of people, men and women, boys and girls, came to watch the strange new game.

31

Then Sweet Medicine cried: "Grandmother, let me hit it once more and make the hoop turn into a fat buffalo calf!" Again he threw his stick like a dart, again the stick went through the center of the hoop, and as it did so the hoop turned into a fat, yellow buffalo calf. The stick had pierced its heart, and the calf fell down dead. "Now you people will have plenty to eat," said Sweet Medicine. "Come and butcher this calf." The people gathered and roasted chunks of tender calf meat over their fires. And no matter how many pieces of flesh they cut from the calf's body, it was never picked clean. However much they ate, there was always more. So the people had their fill, and that was the end of the famine. It was also the first hoop-and-stick game played among the Cheyenne. This sacred game has much power attached to it, and it is still being played.

A boy's first kill is an important happening in his life, something he will always remember. After killing his first buffalo a boy will be honored by his father, who may hold a feast for him and give him a man's name. There would be no such feast for Sweet Medicine, all the same, he was very happy when he killed a fat, yellow calf on his first hunt. He was skinning and butchering it when he was approached by an elderly man, a chief too old to do much hunting, but still harsh and commanding. "This is just the kind of hide I have been looking for," said the chief. "I will take it." "You can't have a boy's first hide." said Sweet Medicine. "Surely you must know this. But you are welcome to half of the meat, because I honor old age." The chief took the meat but grabbed the hide too, and began to walk off with it. Sweet Medicine took hold of one end, and they started a tug-of-war. The chief used his riding whip on Sweet Medicine, shouting: "How dare a poor nothing boy defy a chief?" As he whipped Sweet Medicine again and again across the face, the boy's fighting spirit was aroused. He grabbed a big buffalo leg bone and hit the old man over the head.

Some say Sweet Medicine killed that chief, others say the old man just fell down stunned. But in the village the people were angry that a mere boy had dared to fight the old chief. Some said, "Let's whip him," others said, "Let's kill him." After he had returned to the old woman's lodge, Sweet Medicine sensed what was going on. He said: "Grandmother, some young men of the warrior societies will come here to kill me for having stood up for myself." He thanked her for her kindness to him and then fled from the village. Later when the young warriors came, they were so angry to find the boy gone that they pulled down the lodge and set fire to it.

The following morning someone saw Sweet Medicine, dressed as a Fox warrior, standing on a hill overlooking the village. His enemies set out in pursuit, but he was always just out of their reach and they finally retired exhausted. The next morning he appeared as an Elk warrior, carrying a crooked coupstick wrapped in otter skin. Again, they tried to catch him and kill him, and again he evaded them. They resumed their futile chase on the third morning, when he wore the red face paint and feathers of a Red Shield warrior, and on the fourth, when he dressed like a Dog soldier and shook a small red rattle tied with buffalo hair at his pursuers. On the fifth day he appeared in the full regalia of a Cheyenne chief. That made the village warriors angrier than ever, but they still couldn't catch him, and after that they saw him no more.

Wandering alone over the prairie, the boy heard a voice calling, leading him to a beautiful dark-forested land of many hills. Standing apart from the others was a single mountain shaped like a huge tipi: the sacred mountain called Bear Butte. Sweet Medicine found a secret opening which has since been closed (or perhaps is visible to him alone) and entered the mountain. It was hollow inside like a tipi, forming a sacred lodge filled with people who looked like ordinary men and women, but were really powerful spirits. "Grandson, come in, we have been expecting you, "the holy people said, and when Sweet Medicine took his seat, they began teaching him the Cheyenne way to live so that he could return to the people and give them this knowledge. First of all, the spirits gave him the sacred four arrows, saying, "This is the great gift we are handing you. With these wonderful arrows, the tribe will prosper. Two arrows are for war and two are for hunting. But there is much, much more to the four arrows. They have great powers. They contain rules by which men ought to live."

The spirit people taught Sweet Medicine how to pray to the arrows, how to keep them, how to renew them. They taught him the wise laws of the forty-four chiefs. They taught him how to set up rules for the warrior societies. They taught him how women should be honored. They taught him the many useful things by which people could live, survive, and prosper, things that people had not yet learned at that time. Finally they taught him how to make a special tipi in which the sacred arrows were to be kept. Sweet Medicine listened respectfully and learned well, and finally an old spirit man burned incense of sweet grass to purify both Sweet Medicine and the sacred arrow bundle. Then the Cheyenne boy put the holy bundle on his back and began the long journey home to his people.

During his absence there had been a famine in the land. The buffalo had gone into hiding, for they were angry that the people did not know how to live and were behaving badly. When Sweet Medicine arrived at the village, he found a group of tired and listless children, their ribs sticking out, who were playing with little buffalo figures they had made out of mud. Sweet Medicine immediately changed the figures into large chunks of juicy buffalo meat and fat. "Now there's enough for you to eat," he told the young ones, "with plenty left over for your parents and grandparents. Take the meat, fat, and tongues into the village, and tell two good young hunters to come out in the morning to meet me." Though the children carried the message and two young hunters went out and looked everywhere for Sweet Medicine the next day, all they saw was a big eagle circling above them. They tried again on the second and third days with no success, but on the fourth morning they found Sweet Medicine standing on top of a hill overlooking the village. He told the two: "I have come bringing a wonderful gift from the Creator which the spirits inside the great medicine mountain have sent you. Tell the people to set up a big lodge in the center of the camp circle. Cover its floor with sage, and purify it with burning sweet grass. Tell everyone to go inside the tipi and stay there, no one must see me approaching."

When at last all was made ready, Sweet Medicine walked slowly toward the village and four times called out: "People of the Cheyenne, with a great power I am approaching. Be joyful. The sacred arrows I am bringing." He entered the tipi with the sacred arrow bundle and said: "You have not yet learned the right way to live. That is why the Ones above were angry and the buffalo went into hiding." The two young hunters lit the fire, and Sweet Medicine filled a deer-bone pipe with sacred tobacco. All night through, he taught the people what the spirits inside the holy mountain had taught him. These teachings established the way of the Tsistsistas, the true Cheyenne nation. Toward the morning, Sweet Medicine sang four sacred songs. After each song he smoked the pipe, and its holy breath ascended through the smoke hole up into the sky, up to the great mystery. At daybreak, as the sun rose and the people emerged from the sacred arrow lodge, they found the prairie around them covered with buffalo. The spirits were no longer angry. The famine was over.

For many nights to come, Sweet Medicine instructed the people in the sacred laws. He lived among the Cheyenne for a long time and made them into a proud tribe respected throughout the plains. Four lives the Creator had given him, but even Sweet Medicine was not immortal. Only the rocks and the mountains are forever. When he grew old and feeble and felt that the end of his appointed time was near, he directed the people to carry him to a place near the sacred Bear Butte. There they made a small hut for him out of cottonwood branches and cedar lodge poles covered with bark and leaves. They spread

its floor with sage, flat cedar leaves, and fragrant grass. It was a good lodge to die in, and when they placed him before it, he addressed the people for the last time: "I have seen in my mind that sometime after I am dead...and may the time be long... light-skinned bearded men will arrive with sticks spitting fire. They will conquer the land and drive you before them. They will kill the animals who give you their flesh that you may live, and they will bring strange animals for you to ride and eat. They will introduce war and evil, strange sickness and death. They will try and make you forget Maheo, the Creator, and the things I have taught you, and will impose their own alien, evil ways. They will take your land little by little, until there is nothing left for you. I do not like to tell you this, but you must know. You must be strong when that bad time comes, you men, and particularly you women, because much depends on you, because you are the perpetuators of life and if you weaken, the Cheyenne will cease to be. Now I have said all there is to say."
Then Sweet Medicine went into his hut to die.

(Told by members of the Strange Owl family on the Lame Deer Indian Reservation, Montana, Erdoes, 1967).

As previously mentioned, mountains have always played an important part in the spiritual lives of people. From Mount Everest, Rocky Top, TN, Rocky Mountains, the Appalachian Mountain chain, the coal-rich mountains of West VA, Carpathians, etc., there is a fascination with its splendor and element defying majesty. Perhaps that's the thrill of climbing them, to accomplish and overcome obstacles in our lives, build confidence, or simply to enjoy the view. But there is something holy, majestic and sacred about being on top of a mountain. Perhaps like the Lakota and Cheyenne, this is where most people feel closest to God. In other faiths, such as Judaism and Christianity, there is also a rich history in their scriptures about people who climbed specific mountains to encounter God.

The Story of Moses: Exodus 3

Now Moses was tending the flock of Jethro his father-in-law, the priest of Midian, and he led the flock to the far side of the wilderness and came to Horeb, the mountain of God. There the angel of the LORD appeared to him in flames of fire from within a bush. Moses saw that though the bush was on fire it did not burn up. So Moses thought, "I will go over and see this strange sight—why the bush does not burn up." When the LORD saw that he had gone over to look, God called to him from within the bush, "Moses! Moses!" And Moses said, "Here I am." "Do not come any closer," God said. "Take off your sandals, for the place where you are standing is holy ground." Then he said, "I am the God of your father, the God of Abraham, the God of Isaac and the God of Jacob." At this, Moses hid his face, because he was afraid to look at God.

The LORD said, "I have indeed seen the misery of my people in Egypt. I have heard them crying out because of their slave drivers, and I am concerned about their suffering. So I have come down to rescue them from the hand of the Egyptians and to bring them up out of that land into a good and spacious land, a land flowing with milk and honey—the home of the Canaanites, Hittites, Amorites, Perizzites, Hivites and Jebusites. And now the cry of the Israelites has reached me, and I have seen the way the Egyptians are oppressing them. So now, go. I am sending you to Pharaoh to bring my people the Israelites out of Egypt."

Later, Moses went up on this same mountain to receive the 10 Commandments at Mount Sinai:

On the first day of the third month after the Israelites left Egypt—on that very day—they came to the Desert of Sinai. After they set out from Rephidim, they entered the Desert of Sinai, and Israel camped there in the desert in front of the mountain. Then Moses went up to God, and the LORD called to him from the mountain and said, "This is what you are to say to the descendants of Jacob and what you are to tell the people of Israel: 'You yourselves have seen what I did to Egypt, and how I carried you on eagles' wings and brought you to myself. *⁵ Now if you obey me fully and keep my covenant, then out of all nations you will be my treasured possession. Although the whole earth is mine, you will be for me a kingdom of priests and a holy nation.' These are the words you are to speak to the Israelites."*

So Moses went back and summoned the elders of the people and set before them all the words the LORD had commanded him to speak. The people all responded together, "We will do everything the LORD has said." So Moses brought their answer back to the LORD. The LORD said to Moses, "I am going to come to you in a dense cloud, so that the people will hear me speaking with you and will always put their trust in you." Then Moses told the LORD what the people had said. And the LORD said to Moses, "Go to the people and consecrate them today and tomorrow. Have them wash their clothes and be ready by the third day, because on that day the LORD will come down on Mount Sinai in the sight of all the people. Put limits for the people around the mountain and tell them, 'Be careful that you do not approach the mountain or touch the foot of it. Whoever touches the mountain is to be put to death. They are to be stoned or shot with arrows; not a hand is to be laid on them. No person or animal shall be permitted to live.' Only when the ram's horn sounds a long blast may they approach the mountain." After Moses had gone down the mountain to the people, he consecrated them, and they washed their clothes. Then he said to the people, "Prepare yourselves for the third day. Abstain from sexual relations."

On the morning of the third day there was thunder and lightning, with a thick cloud over the mountain, and a very loud trumpet blast. Everyone in the camp trembled. Then Moses led the people out of the camp to meet with God, and they stood at the foot of the mountain. Mount Sinai was covered with smoke, because the LORD descended on it in fire. The smoke billowed up from it like smoke from a furnace, and the whole mountain trembled violently. As the sound of the trumpet grew louder and louder, Moses spoke and the voice of God answered him. The

Lord descended to the top of Mount Sinai and called Moses to the top of the mountain. So Moses went up and the LORD said to him, "Go down and warn the people so they do not force their way through to see the LORD and many of them perish. Even the priests, who approach the LORD, must consecrate themselves, or the LORD will break out against them." Moses said to the LORD, "The people cannot come up Mount Sinai, because you yourself warned us, 'Put limits around the mountain and set it apart as holy.'"

Elsewhere, Elijah the prophet encountered the Lord on Mount Carmel: 1 Kings 18

So Obadiah went to meet Ahab and told him, and Ahab went to meet Elijah. When he saw Elijah, he said to him, "Is that you, you troubler of Israel?" "I have not made trouble for Israel," Elijah replied. "But you and your father's family have. You have abandoned the LORD's commands and have followed the Baals. Now summon the people from all over Israel to meet me on Mount Carmel. And bring the four hundred and fifty prophets of Baal and the four hundred prophets of Asherah, who eat at Jezebel's table." So Ahab sent word throughout all Israel and assembled the prophets on Mount Carmel. Elijah went before the people and said, "How long will you waver between two opinions? If the LORD is God, follow him; but if Baal is God, follow him." But the people said nothing.
Then Elijah said to them, "I am the only one of the LORD's prophets left, but Baal has four hundred and fifty prophets. Get

two bulls for us. Let Baal's prophets choose one for themselves, and let them cut it into pieces and put it on the wood but not set fire to it. I will prepare the other bull and put it on the wood but not set fire to it. Then you call on the name of your god, and I will call on the name of the LORD. The god who answers by fire—he is God."

Then all the people said, "What you say is good." Elijah said to the prophets of Baal, "Choose one of the bulls and prepare it first, since there are so many of you. Call on the name of your god, but do not light the fire." So they took the bull given them and prepared it. Then they called on the name of Baal from morning till noon. "Baal, answer us!" they shouted. But there was no response; no one answered. And they danced around the altar they had made.

At noon Elijah began to taunt them. "Shout louder!" he said. "Surely he is a god! Perhaps he is deep in thought, or busy, or traveling. Maybe he is sleeping and must be awakened." So they shouted louder and slashed themselves with swords and spears, as was their custom, until their blood flowed. Midday passed, and they continued their frantic prophesying until the time for the evening sacrifice. But there was no response, no one answered, no one paid attention. Then Elijah said to all the people, "Come here to me." They came to him, and he repaired the altar of the LORD, which had been torn down. Elijah took twelve stones, one for each of the tribes descended from Jacob, to whom the word of the LORD had come, saying, "Your name shall be Israel." With the stones he built an altar in the name of the LORD, and he dug a trench around it large enough to hold two seahs of seed. He arranged the wood, cut the bull into pieces and laid it on the wood. Then he said to them, "Fill four large jars with water and pour it on the offering and on the wood. Do it again," he said, and they did it again. "Do it a third time," he ordered, and they did it the third time. The water ran down around the altar and even filled the trench.

At the time of sacrifice, the prophet Elijah stepped forward and prayed: "LORD, the God of Abraham, Isaac and Israel, let it be known today that you are God in Israel and that I am your servant and have done all these things at your command. Answer me, LORD, answer me, so these people will know that you, LORD, are God, and that you are turning their hearts back again."

Then the fire of the LORD fell and burned up the sacrifice, the wood, the stones and the soil, and also licked up the water in the trench. When all the people saw this, they fell prostrate and cried, "The LORD—he is God! The LORD—he is God!"

In the New Testament section of the Bible, Jesus twice used the sacredness of a mountain as a deeper lesson in spiritual connection:

The Transfiguration of Jesus: Matthew 17

After six days Jesus took with him Peter, James and John the brother of James, and led them up a high mountain by themselves. There he was transfigured before them. His face shone like the sun, and his clothes became as white as the

43

light. Just then there appeared before them Moses and Elijah, talking with Jesus. Peter said to Jesus, "Lord, it is good for us to be here. If you wish, I will put up three shelters—one for you, one for Moses and one for Elijah." While he was still speaking, a bright cloud covered them, and a voice from the cloud said, "This is my Son, whom I love; with him I am well pleased. Listen to him!" When the disciples heard this, they fell facedown to the ground, terrified. But Jesus came and touched them. "Get up," he said. "Don't be afraid." When they looked up, they saw no one except Jesus.

Jesus Talks With a Samaritan Woman: John 4:1-26

Now Jesus learned that the Pharisees had heard that he was gaining and baptizing more disciples than John— although in fact it was not Jesus who baptized, but his disciples. So he left Judea and went back once more to Galilee. Now he had to go through Samaria. So he came to a town in Samaria called Sychar, near the plot of ground Jacob had given to his son Joseph.

Jacob's well was there, and Jesus, tired as he was from the journey, sat down by the well. It was about noon. When a Samaritan woman came to draw water, Jesus said to her, "Will you give me a drink?" (His disciples had gone into the town to buy food.) The Samaritan woman said to him, "You are a Jew and I am a Samaritan woman. How can you ask me for a drink?" (For Jews do not associate with Samaritans.) Jesus answered her, "If you knew the gift of God and who it is that asks you for a drink, you would have asked him and he would have given you living water." "Sir," the woman said, "you have nothing to draw with and the well is deep. Where can you get this living water? Are you greater than our father Jacob, who gave us the well and drank from it himself, as did also his sons and his livestock?"

Jesus answered, "Everyone who drinks this water will be thirsty again, but whoever drinks the water I give them will never thirst. Indeed, the water I give them will become in them a spring of water welling up to eternal life." The woman said to him, "Sir, give me this water so that I won't get thirsty and have to keep coming here to draw water." He told her, "Go, call your husband and come back." "I have no husband," she replied. Jesus said to her, "You are right when you say you have no husband. The fact is, you have had five husbands, and the man you now have is not your husband. What you have just said is quite true."

"Sir," the woman said, "I can see that you are a prophet. Our ancestors worshiped on this mountain, but you Jews claim that the place where we must worship is in Jerusalem." "Woman," Jesus replied, "believe me, a time is coming when you will worship the Father neither on this mountain nor in Jerusalem. You Samaritans worship what you do not know; we worship what we do know, for salvation is from the Jews. Yet a time is coming and has now come when the true worshipers will worship the Father in the Spirit and in truth, for they are the kind of worshipers the Father seeks. God is spirit, and his worshipers must worship in the Spirit and in truth." The

woman said, "I know that Messiah" (called Christ) "is coming. When he comes, he will explain everything to us." Then Jesus declared, "I, the one speaking to you—I am he."

It has been my experience as a mental health therapist, teacher, and pastor that psycho-spiritual transformation involves both a personal transformation, i.e., a movement that draws us inward to ourselves; and a personal transcendence, a movement that draws us beyond ourselves and our limitations. It is worth noting that the ancient Greek word *ekstasis*, literally means "to step outside of oneself." Ironically, to acknowledge something and someone greater than ourselves often fans the flame to go beyond ourselves in spite of circumstances and feelings of doubt. Yet, therein lies unlimited possibilities, a lifelong journey as it were, capable of causing ripples across centuries for generations to discover. Interestingly, we find a similarity in our word for "church." *Ekklesia* is translated in the New Testament as the people who are called out of this fatalistic worldly nature and endless pursuits of things that never satisfy, and into a spiritual realm desiring to experience that which has kissed the soul. This understanding has often been the source of tension as despite the vast aesthetic value, the history the "people of God" were never intended to be a physical building or permanent structure. In the Christian sense, Church was (and will always) intended to be a living, breathing, life-changing, spirit to Spirit, flesh and blood people who have been transformed by God's Spirit through the life, death and resurrection of Christ. In fact, over the last quarter century, I have noticed that more and more people are reclaiming authenticity outside the bounds of a place and finding it in relationships not defined by brick and mortar structures.

In the Old Testament, the word "to know" comes from the Hebrew root Yada' (*yah-daw*), and occurs approximately 873 times! Based on its sheer repetition is something I believe we should be paying attention to more closely. Here is a break-down of where *Yada* occurs in the books of the Old Testament:

Genesis	52	Exodus	43	Leviticus	9	Numbers	17
Deuteronomy	43	Joshua	15	Judges	21	Ruth	8
1 Samuel	51	2 Samuel	28	1 Kings	29	2 Kings	16
1 Chronicles	8	2 Chronicles	17	Esther	9	Nehemiah	7
Job	69	Psalms	91	Ecclesiastes	30	Song of Solomon	2
Isaiah	64	Jeremiah	62	Ezekiel	97	Daniel	7
Hosea	14	Joel	3	Amos	4	Jonah	6
Micah	3	Nahum	2	Habakkuk	2	Zephaniah	1
Zechariah	9	Malachi	1				

Hebrew scholars Brown, Driver and Briggs (1979) define Yada' as to acknowledge, acquainted with, advise, answer, appoint, assuredly, be aware. To know is also used in a great variety of senses, figuratively, literally, euphemistically and inferentially (including observation, care, recognition; and causatively, instruction, designation, punishment, etc.). There is an acknowledgement, acquaintance(-ted with), advise, answer, appoint, assuredly, be aware, certainly, comprehend, consider, cunning, declare, be diligent, discern, discover, endued with, familiar friend, famous, feel, can have, be ignorant, instruct, kinsfolk, kinsman, know, come to give or take knowledge, have

JAMES A. HOUCK JR., PhD

knowledge, make known, mark, perceive, privy to, regard, have respect, skillful, of a surety, teach, tell, understand. Finally, *yada* is to know another in a relational sense, to recognize, be acquainted with and to understand our existence in relation even to God.

In the New Testament *ginosko, eido,* and *epiginosko* are the three most frequent Greek words to describe "know." Throughout the 27 books of the New Testament, "to know", "be known", "to see" and "to understand" (in various forms) are used over 500 times (Wigram, 1979). All of these words convey an encouragement to our faith so that we may experience the fullness of all that God intends for us to have. For example, *ginosko* appears in the following books:

Matthew	20	Mark	12	Luke	28	John	49
Acts	16	Romans	9	1 Corinthians	13	2 Corinthians	7
Galatians	3	Ephesians	3	Philippians	5	Colossians	1
1 Thessalonians	1	2 Timothy	3	Hebrews	4	James	3
2 Peter	2	1 John	21	2 John	1	Revelation	4

It is no accident that both John's gospel and the first epistle that bears his name contain more references to *ginosko* than any other New Testament book. For John, *knowing* God in Christ was/is not about a solely intellectual discovery but rather encapsulates a combination of a person's experience, intimacy, devotion and love for God (Brown, 2003). Furthermore, it was John who refers to himself as *the disciple whom Jesus loved* (John 13:23, 19:26, 20:2, 21:24) in the gospel and wanted others to experience the same authentic relationship that he delighted in with Christ:

That which was from the beginning, which we have heard, which we have seen with our eyes, which we have looked at and our hands have touched—this we proclaim concerning the Word of life. The life appeared; we have seen it and testify to it, and we proclaim to you the eternal life, which was with the Father and has appeared to us. We proclaim to you what we have seen and heard, so that you also may have fellowship with us. And our fellowship is with the Father and with his Son, Jesus Christ. We write this to make our joy complete.

1 John 1:1-4

John Wesley (1703-1791), founder of Methodism, also understood the limitations of knowing God exclusively through reasoning:

Reason, however cultivated and improved, cannot produce the love of God. It cannot produce either faith or hope; from which alone this love can flow. It is only then that we behold by faith what manner of love the Father has bestowed upon us, in giving his only Son, that we might not perish but have everlasting life. . .let reason do all that reason can: employ it as far as it will go. But at the same time, acknowledge it is utterly incapable of giving either faith, or hope, or love; and consequently, of producing either real virtue, or substantial happiness.

(The Sermons of John Wesley-1872 edition).

Similar to John the Apostle, Wesley's desire to know the fullness of God was placed in a tangible, experiential relationship. For example, he wrote in his journal about a particular night in which he encountered God filling something in him that he was lacking:

> *In the evening I went very unwillingly to a society in Aldersgate Street, where one was reading Luther's preface to the Epistle to the Romans. About a quarter before nine, while the leader was describing the change which God works in the heart through faith in Christ, I felt my heart strangely warmed. I felt I did trust in Christ alone for salvation; and an assurance was given me that He had taken away my sins, even mine, and saved me from the law of sin and death.*

In our own search to reclaim our authenticity, psycho-spiritual transformation also draws us out of this world as we are drawn inwardly towards the everlasting love of God. Christian author James R. Beck (1999) states that what we are actually drawn to is the *agape* love of God (a love that does not seek to get something for itself, but rather seeks to fill something missing in another), because it was this kind of love that drew (and draws) Christ to us. In fact, it was the very intention of God for Christ's life, death and resurrection to transform and fill in us the very thing we lack in ourselves: *To experience the fullness of God's unconditional love and to fully embrace the uniqueness of who we are.* In a sense, we love and are loved; we know and we are known, see and are seen.

Being able to fully comprehend the *agape* love of God is difficult for us to grasp, let alone live out on a daily basis. It is difficult not impossible. To live out *agape* love challenges us to set aside our linear thinking and our egos, and focus on fulfilling another person's needs before our own. To be quite honest, we are perhaps more comfortable living out *phileo* love, i.e., a brotherly or sisterly type of love that seeks to get something from others which we lack in ourselves. In other words, our egos often dictate our behavior as *phileo* love draws us to other people in order to get our physical, emotional even spiritual needs met, not theirs; and vice versa. On one level, this inter-dependence is not necessarily a negative thing since we do rely on each other for food, clothing, shelter, medical care, companionship, income, emotional support, etc. However, the more we experience the *agape* love of God on a palpable, personal level, the more intently we are drawn to living authentically. In fact, it was with this very intention of wanting to experience the height, depth, width and breadth of God's *agape* love for me that I set out on my own psycho-spiritual journey to reclaim my authentic self.

Strapping on the Proverbial Seatbelt: My Story

Rarely is a journey just a journey. The miles we travel are often filled with anticipation, assumptions, and attitudes about what lies ahead. Excitement often swells our hearts (and at times our heads) as we ask: *What will I find? What will it be like? How long will it take? Am I there yet?* However, instead of sitting back and enjoying the ride, we become fixated on answering these questions. In fact, we may often lose sight of the transformative purpose of the journey itself. Still, we may be in the habit of asking these questions of who, what, when, where and why, because of our past experiences. Indeed, where we have come from and where we have been, often influences us on where we think we want to go on this journey and what we will find.

But let us consider this thought: If we behave this way when we take a physical trip, are we just as curious, anxious, and impatient about our own spiritual journey? After all, we may not take into consideration the stamina and fortitude needed to undertake such a trip; it is not a journey of haste but of self-discovery, integration and endurance. In fact, we do not take such a psycho-spiritual journey alone. As Hebrews 12:1-3 reminds us:

> *Therefore, since we are surrounded by such a great cloud of witnesses, let us throw off everything that hinders and the sin that so easily entangles. And let us run with perseverance the race marked out for us, fixing our eyes on Jesus, the pioneer and perfecter of faith. For the joy set before him he endured the cross, scorning its shame, and sat down at the right hand of the throne of God. Consider him who endured such opposition from sinners, so that you will not grow weary and lose heart.*

Psycho-spiritual journeys have often been misunderstood as having a linear or logical sequence, containing a specific beginning and ending point. Instead, a psycho-spiritual journey is far less defined. We may point to a specific time when we realized we are seeking a psycho-spiritual path, but quite often, this kind of journey takes us into ourselves and beyond ourselves. At times the journey circles back and present us with life lessons we have yet to learn. They are open-ended, unknown, and even mysterious. Psycho-spiritual journeys require a faith that takes us beyond our personal assumptive boundaries. They take us out of our comfort zones and limitations. They take us to self-discovery and wonder; not so much about how far we have come, but more in terms how far we have yet to go. In fact, we never should believe that we have arrived or reached the end of our journey while on this earth. To our surprise, these journeys are more about grappling with our authenticity via the recognition of how God uses irony in our lives. In fact, however uncertain we are about what lies ahead we can take comfort by the fact that we are never alone. We are in full view of millions and millions of people who have gone before us. We are connected to our ancestors by our humanity and the relentless desire to pursue the One who has called our name. Our stories connect with theirs as one continuous narrative of ironic encounters with ourselves, others and God. Perhaps it is this element of irony where we first begin to see God in our lives.

Indeed, one of the most popular genres in literature is irony. Defined as *an outcome or result of an event/experience contrary to what was, or might have been, expected.* Irony invokes a wide range of feelings in us from shock and surprise to anger, disappointment, and everything in between. Today, many people confuse irony with an unfortunate set of circumstances. For example, let's say that you have spent months planning a family reunion. You have e-mailed all the invitations, dug out your favorite barbeque recipes and spent a small fortune on the ingredients. You have reserved a pavilion at the state park complete with public hiking trails and horseshoe pits. However, on the day of the reunion there is a torrential downpour that makes it impossible to go to the park. Is it ironic? No. It is simply unfortunate that it rains the day of your reunion. Of course you always have the option of moving the festivities inside. At least the food will not go to waste and you have a chance to spend quality time with your extended family. Just explain to Uncle Joe that there is no horseshoe pitching in the basement!

Irony, on the other hand, comes with a purposeful lesson attached to it. In fact, irony has a way to teach us those life-changing lessons, if we are willing to listen to its message and understand what it requires from us: For me, regardless of the circumstances, it is all about the journey not the destination. Whenever I watch a movie or read a book that involves a group of people going from one place to another, in my mind I strap on the proverbial seatbelt and hang on for the ride! I know that although the characters are destined to complete their trip, the real journey occurs on the inside of each person. For example, in the movie *The Wizard of Oz*, Dorothy and her three companions seek the Wizard in order that he might grant them what they believe they lack. The tin man needed a heart. The scarecrow needed a brain. The cowardly lion needed courage. And of course, Dorothy wanted to go home. Their journey is filled with dangerous encounters and harrowing escapes from the Wicked Witch of the West and her minions. After the Witch was defeated, as the Wizard commanded, and all was well, the four companions go back to the Wizard to receive their rewards. The Wizard then takes them back in time and explains that through their ordeal, they each displayed what they lacked. The tin man displayed tremendous heart of devotion and loyalty. The scarecrow turned out to be the "brains" of the outfit. The cowardly lion showed remarkable courage in the face of overwhelming odds. And Dorothy, as we all know, had the ability to go home anytime she wanted. She finally realized that there was no other place more magical than her own home and those who loved her.

A psycho-spiritual journey can be like this too. Buddhist nun, author and teacher, Pema Chodron notes that *embarking on a journey is like getting into a very small boat and setting out on the ocean to search for unknown lands.* How many times do we desire to go in search of something deeper and more meaningful in our relationship with God, only to realize that we may have been looking for what we already have? All that was needed was for it to be realized and reclaimed as our own.

I used to question that the whole transformation and transcendence subject was similar to the "chicken-egg" debate. Which comes first? Are we transformed by God's grace and then we are able to transcend ourselves, or is it in transcending ourselves and limitations that we become transformed? I believe it doesn't matter. Transformation and transcendence is an on-going dance as it were; a continuous weave of experiences whereby you lose track of the common thread woven throughout, but you know it is in there nonetheless. Despite different changes we see in our lives (which others often acknowledge in us first) there is a need to address underlying issues that may have contributed to our emotional/spiritual problems in the first place. This requires a person to shift his/her attitudes, behaviors, personal relationships and even communities. Moreover, this change extends to more than just eliminating behaviors and attitudes, but also taking on healthier patterns of living and to live a more authentic, harmonious life.

When we experience psycho-spiritual transformation, we become aware of how much we long for more of God's presence in our lives. God's Spirit sparks an authentic spiritual hunger and thirst in us that causes our soul to never be satisfied with anything less that is not authentic, genuine and real. Perhaps this is why we are encouraged to seek the Lord with all our heart soul mind and strength (Deuteronomy 6:5, Luke 10:27). As Psalm 42 states:

> As the deer pants for streams of water, so my soul pants for you, my God. My soul thirsts for God, for the living God. When can I go and meet with God? My tears have been my food day and night, while people say to me all day long, "Where is your God?" These things I remember as I pour out my soul: how I used to go to the house of God under

the protection of the Mighty One with shouts of joy
and praise among the festive throng. Why, my soul,
are you downcast? Why so disturbed within me?
Put your hope in God, for I will yet praise him, my
Savior and my God.

Several years ago I found myself becoming interested in being a "bridge person", one who walks between two cultures by looking for connections that could bring unity, understanding and healing for both (Sun Bear, 1987). Even before I had ever heard of this term, I have always found a resonating compatibility between Native American spirituality and my own Christian faith. In fact, it is through understanding another's religion and spirituality that I have come to better understand my own. For example, my own faith has been enhanced by Native American traditions that celebrate God as the Creator and Sustainer of this world. Through native songs, dances and other traditions, I have discovered a stronger connection to all living things, as well as my responsibilities of stewardship to care for all that have been gifted to humanity. I am not alone in this discovery. Certainly, these and other similar beliefs have been celebrated among Christian and Native Americans (Stolzman, 1995). Unfortunately, I am also aware of history which has also revealed times of Christianity's extreme prejudice, intolerance, and strong-armed conversions toward native people, which still contributes to intergenerational post-traumatic stress and internalized oppression among Native Americans to this day (Duran, 1995).

The initial steps to reclaiming my authentic self led me to my own psycho-spiritual retreat to Bear Butte, South Dakota. As previously mentioned, Bear Butte, or *Mathó Pahá*, is considered a scared place among the Cheyenne and Lakota people. I was drawn to this mountain because prominent Native American Chiefs such as Red Cloud, Crazy Horse, Sweet Medicine, Sitting Bull and Frank Fools Crow, all made pilgrimages to this mountain to seek God's (*Wakan Tanka* in Sioux) will for their lives and the lives of their communities. Bear Butte was and is also an important site for the Sioux and Cheyenne vision quest in which the seeker finds a solitary place on the mountain to pray, dream, meditate, sing and cry out for a transformative vision from God. Since its peak rises over 1,200 feet above the surrounding plain, climbing Bear Butte was no small journey. But then again, any spiritual journey that involves both the external and internal is no small feat. I stood at the base of the mountain for the longest time, remembering the stories I was told about this site. I had traveled a great distance and my expectations were high. I also imagined the number of footprints that have trotted its soil and how many prayers had been offered by countless native generations.

After quietly saying my own prayer of gratitude, I started to hike the twisting trail on an ever increasing incline. I remembered how focused I was on getting to the top. For me, reaching the summit was the end of my journey, or so I thought. After all, everyone I talked to said that the best part of the climb was reaching the top; a place where one can see for miles and miles in any direction. I would stop occasionally along the way and rest, take a look around, sip some water, and admire the view. Nevertheless, I reminded myself that I needed to keep going if I wanted to reach the peak. Along the way, I met fellow hikers coming down the mountain, and of course like many ascending hikers I asked, *"How much further?"* The response was always the same: *"You're at such and such a point, but hang in there, when you get to the top, it's worth it. The view is spectacular. Like nothing you've ever seen!"* Fueled by these words of encouragement I kept hiking. Finally, I reached the top of the mountain. I now understood what they meant: The journey was indeed worth it! I stood on a wooden platform and held a spectacular view in four directions. The air was cool and breezy, and spoke a kind of whispering melody as it blew through the colorful tobacco ties that lined the long-needle pine trees. I sat there for the longest time just absorbing beauty like I had never seen. In a quiet humility I thanked God for His majesty and splendor of creation. No other words were necessary. In fact, more words would have spoiled the experience. Instead it felt as though my spirit was speaking directly to the God's Spirit. Now I understood why Native Americans consider Bear Butte a sacred place! I wanted to stay up there forever bathed in that spiritual presence. I also understood how Peter must have felt when he was on the Mount of Transfiguration with Jesus:

> *I think it is right to refresh your memory as long as*
> *I live in the tent of this body, because I know that I*
> *will soon put it aside, as our Lord Jesus Christ has*
> *made clear to me. And I will make every effort to*

see that after my departure you will always be able to remember these things. For we did not follow cleverly devised stories when we told you about the coming of our Lord Jesus Christ in power, but we were eyewitnesses of his majesty. He received honor and glory from God the Father when the voice came to him from the Majestic Glory, saying, "This is my Son, whom I love; with him I am well pleased." We ourselves heard this voice that came from heaven when we were with him on the sacred mountain.

2 Peter 1:13–18

After what seemed like hours on the mountain top, the time had come for me to descend. Little did I know that my good friend irony was waiting for the right moment to teach me what I had failed to see all this time. As I hiked down the mountain (much faster now than ascending), I met other hikers coming up. To my surprise they also asked the question, *"How much further?"* To which I replied, *"You're about half-way or two-thirds of the way up, but hang in there, it's worth it. The view is spectacular. Like nothing you've ever seen!"* No sooner had I wished my fellow hikers well, and taken a couple of steps, then it hit me: I had missed the whole point of the journey! Although my goal was to climb to the top of the mountain, I had forgotten the most basic lesson of all. . .seeing the beauty of the mountain along the way. Indeed, the journey itself is where the real transformation occurs. I was so preoccupied with the end that I had missed the lessons along the way; lessons that appeared to me with every step I took. Ironically, we find the same lesson in our psycho-spiritual journeys: Sometimes we get so focused on getting to heaven someday (the goal) that we missed the opportunities (the process) when God is right beside us each day; subtle ways in which the Spirit's presence speaks to us in creation, relationships, even chaos and grief. Remember that famous Parable of the Sheep and the Goats? *"Lord, when did we see you hungry, thirsty, a stranger, naked, sick or imprisoned?"* If truth be told, perhaps there are times we never see the Lord in everyday circumstances either, because we are not even looking for Him? (Matthew 25:31-46)

Despite the fact that we are capable of accomplishing many wonderful things in our lives, we cannot go from one experience to another without something changing or transforming in us. We are forever changed by our experiences. This is not only the ironic message of the Wizard of Oz, but also grounded in the good news of Jesus Christ. No matter where Christ went in his life, or where people travel today, there are people wondering where God fits into their lives? Questions such as, *Do I have a place in the gospel message? Can the gospel message find a place in me? Does God love me? Can God, others and I forgive me for all I have done, and does my faith, religion and spirituality allow me to be an authentic person?* These are all poignant and relevant questions because they strike at the very heart of our need to reclaim our genuineness and authenticity.

Nevertheless, if we are open to the lessons that God teaches us through irony we will be surprised to find how often we look for authenticity in an inauthentic world of conditional love. In his book entitled *The Return of the Prodigal Son,* Nouwen

(1994) zeroes in on this futile search for things that simply cannot satisfy the ache of our soul:

> *At issue here is the question: "To whom do I belong? God or to the world?" Many of my daily preoccupations suggest that I belong more to the world than to God. A little criticism makes me angry, and a little rejection makes me depressed. A little praise raises my spirits, and a little success excites me. It takes very little to raise me up or thrust me down. Often I am like a small boat on the ocean, completely at the mercy of its waves. All the time and energy I spend in keeping some kind of balance and preventing myself from being tipped over and drowning shows that my life is mostly a struggle for survival: not a holy struggle, but an anxious struggle resulting from the mistaken idea that it is the world that defines me.*

> *However, as long as I keep running about asking: "Do you love me? Do you really love me?" I give all power to the voices of the world and put myself in bondage because the world is filled with "ifs." The world says: "Yes, I love you if you are good-looking, intelligent, and wealthy. I love you if you have a good education, a good job, and good connections. I love you if you produce much, sell much, and buy much." There are endless "ifs" hidden in the world's love. These "ifs" enslave me, since it is impossible to respond adequately to all of them. The*

*world's love is and always will be conditional. As
long as I keep looking for my true self in the world
of conditional love, I will remain "hooked" to the
world-trying, failing, and trying again. It is a world
that fosters addictions because what it offers cannot
satisfy the deepest craving of my heart.*

The Ironic World of Assumptions

Legend has it that once you have reached the top of Bear Butte
you are supposed to leave a piece of yourself behind in order to
take away something better. Because Bear Butte is considered
a Native American sacred place for the living, people are
discouraged from leaving the scattered remains of deceased
loved ones. Nonetheless, there is an inherent wisdom to leaving
something of you behind. The piece of you left behind might be
something in a literal, physical sense, such as a piece of jewelry
or other personal token of significance, or in a metaphorical
sense such as past psycho-spiritual wounds. I believe it means
both. Being on that sacred mountain I saw many physical signs
of what people left behind: prayer ties filled with tobacco,
sacred hoops, dream catchers, various colored cloths filled
with sage or other herbs, and feathers attached to trees. These
tokens might represent prayers of gratitude, thanksgiving,
intercession, petition and other acts of worshipping the Creator
and Sustainer of Life. Regardless, these personal tokens all
displayed a hallowed beauty as they gently swayed in the wind.
For myself, I cannot tell you what I left behind; that is between

the seeker and God. Nevertheless, I can share what I came away with: A renewed sense of seeing the sacredness in all life and relationships. I sensed a connectedness to all living things like never before. In fact, that experience instilled in me a more profound spiritual transformation that compels me to transcend my own worldview of assumptions and limitations.

Assimilation and Accommodation: Internalizing our experiences

From the time we are born we are constantly taking in information via our senses. Indeed, our limited world view consists of what we see, hear, smell, feel and yes, taste. Still, our perspectives are shaped by how we process that information where we learn about our world and internalize our experiences. Employed at the Binet Institute in the 1920s, *Jean Piaget* (1896-1980) began his career in intelligence testing. Assigned to develop French versions of questions on English intelligence tests, Piaget became interested in how children and adults differ in their use of logical thinking. As a result, he became the first psychologist to make a systematic study of cognitive development, namely through *assimilation* (making sense of new experiences based on previously known information) and *accommodation* (making the mental room for newly acquired knowledge).

For example, perhaps a two-year old child comes across a magnet lying on the floor. Notwithstanding the need to baby-proof the home from things that might cause harm to the child, he/she picks up the magnet and proceeds to place it in his/her mouth. Since the early stages of a child's world of experiences is restricted to the mouth, and everything else has been put into the child's mouth, this is how the two-year old will try to understand what this object is (assimilation). An adult on the other hand, sees the child's behavior and immediately takes away the magnet from the child saying, *"Don't put that dirty thing in your mouth!"* Hopefully at this point the adult has something else to give the child, like say a popsicle (unless of course you enjoy hearing a two-year old scream!). Anyway, the child has yet to learn that a magnet is not meant to be eaten. Until this truth is understood, the magnet will be off-limits. *Accommodation*, on the other hand, states that once the child realizes (or makes the mental room for this new understanding) that a magnet can be attached to metal, he/she will be delighted to see how a magnet secures beautifully colored refrigerator art on display for all to see in the future. As the child gets older he/she may discover even more creative new uses for a magnet, such as running it across his/her braces adding to the orthodontist bill!

In addition to *Assimilation* and *Accommodation*, Piaget's other contributions also included a theory of cognitive/intellectual child development, detailed observational studies of cognition in children, and a series of simple tests to reveal their different cognitive abilities (Piaget, 1932). Prior to his work, it was widely held that children were merely less competent thinkers than adults. However, Piaget showed that young children think in strikingly different ways when compared to adults. According to Piaget, children are born with a very basic inherited mental structure on which all future acquiring knowledge is based (Ibid, 1932). Piaget discovered that as they interact with more of their world, children develop more complex cognitive skills. As a result, Piaget theorized his four stages of cognitive development:

- Sensorimotor: Birth through ages 18-24 months.
  Infants focus on what they see, what they are doing, and physical interactions with their immediate environment. They are constantly experimenting with activities such as shaking or throwing things, putting things in their mouths, and learning about the world through trial and error.

- Preoperational: Toddlerhood (18-24 months) through early childhood (age 7).
  During this stage, young children are able to think about things symbolically. Language, memory and imagination develops, which allows them to understand the difference between past and future, and engage in make-believe.

- Concrete operational: Ages 7 to 12, elementary-age and preadolescent children.
  Children's thinking develops beyond themselves as they become increasingly aware of their environment. They begin to realize that their thoughts and feelings are unique and may not be shared by others, or may not even be part of reality.

- Formal operational. Adolescence through adulthood. Adolescents are able to logically use symbols related to abstract concepts, such as algebra and science. They can think about multiple variables in systematic ways, formulate hypotheses, and consider possibilities. They also can ponder abstract relationships and concepts such as justice.

Still, Piaget's theory of Adaptation and Accommodation was and is not just for children. Assimilation and Accommodation are a life-long process of learning for everyone. In fact, we go through this process all the time, from learning to drive a car and raising a family, to being trained on a new piece of equipment at work, learning a new computer system, adjusting to a new phase in life such as retirement and death. We even engage in assimilation and accommodation when we integrate our psycho-spiritual experiences. Furthermore, our perspectives are shaped by how we process information where we learn about our assumptions and internalize our experiences. In other words, when we have a profound psycho-spiritual experience, we are compelled to ask: *"Do we have the courage to seek that unknown potential the experience has awakened in us? Are we willing to change from what is known and comfortable to something that is new and fresh?"* An anonymous sage once said: *"To seek our potential by risking change is the path of true greatness. Such action brings great favor and untold blessing."*

Another contemporary of Piaget, Lev Vygotsky (1896-1934) took a different approach to cognitive learning in that he stressed the importance of social interaction in the development of cognition, even to the point of making meaning in our lives. In fact, he believed that we should never underestimate the role our community plays in the process of creating meaning for each other. For example, when we were children we learned about strategies, skills and, of course, relationships through the interaction with families, friends, teachers, mentors, etc. These people in our lives modeled behaviors for us, as well as instructed us verbally. All of this interaction, Vygotsky says, occurs in a social/cultural context. As a result, it is within this context that we then learn to internalize the lessons, messages, and perceptions that guide our behavior. To further illustrate Vygotsky's point, Shaffer (1996) illustrates a classic analogy of a young girl who receives her first jigsaw puzzle. At first she struggles to fit the pieces together in order to replicate the picture on the box cover. By herself she may be unable to grasp the strategy involved in solving jigsaw puzzles, namely to complete the outside frame of the puzzle first. She needs her father to sit down with her and show her some basic strategies, such as finding all the corner/edge pieces and providing a couple of pieces for the child to put together herself before she realizes the strategy. After some initial words of encouragement, the young girl becomes more competent, and the father allows her to work more independently. Soon she is able to put together many puzzles of increasing difficulty. As a result, she learns to transfer this confidence and skill to more learning challenges in her life as she matures. A word of caution here: Even though learning is a life-long process, we must be careful not to become complacent with what we know, set in our ways, or closed off to new ideas and/or advances in technology. Every new experience, whether we are moving from Piaget's assimilation to accommodation, or Vygotsky's social learning, requires us to examine our assumptions that hinder our desire for change.

From day one, we are thrust into a world of assumptions. We were read bed-time stories of Cinderella, Rapunzel, Snow White, Hansel and Gretel, or one of the other 209 fairy tales from the Brothers Grimm. As children we marvel at the magical ways the stories unfold in our dreams: Adventures to be undertaken, riddles to be solved, challenges to be won, and of course, in the end, all things work out and people typically live happily ever after. Perhaps it is not until after we are older that we are stunned by the amount of violence and crudity found in these tales, but also, subtle assumptions about who we are, what other people are like, and how life is "suppose" to turn out has been forever etched in our memories. As children we soak up these stories of a perfect world where evil is always thwarted, right always triumphs, people find true love and eventually walk hand in hand into a glorious sunset of peace and tranquility. Of course, it does not take us long to discover that the world does not necessarily operate according to the Brothers Grimm, Mother Goose and Dr. Seuss. Admittedly, there are times when injustices occur, innocent people are killed, and the vulnerable are not saved in the nick of time. It is during such times when we may stand bewildered, perplexed, and stunned trying to make sense of our experiences based on what we have been taught, know and assume.

According to personal growth teacher Don Miguel Ruiz (1997), the problem with assumptions is that we tend to believe they are true because we take things personally about other people's attitudes, thoughts and behaviors believed to be directed at us. We often misinterpret and misunderstand these events because we interpret (and then project) them exclusively from our perspective. For example, imagine just how many assumptions we are capable of constructing about another driver who cuts us off in traffic. By their so-called "impulsive actions", we might experience feelings of fear, terror and road rage. In a spilt second, images of accidents, pain, disfigurement, increased insurance premiums, disability, loss of loved-ones, even death may flash in our minds. Furthermore, we may even take their actions personally as if we did something to provoke the behavior such as driving too cautiously on unfamiliar roads or less than ideal weather conditions. Nevertheless, as a result of other drivers' behavior, we may *assume* they are evil. We may *assume* they are rude and impatient and the cause of all accidents in the world. We may even *assume* that all people of their age group drive similar ways and in similar vehicles. We may curse them under our breath or out loud, giving voice to our assumptions about them as a person of a certain age, ethnicity, gender, socio-economic factors, etc. But wait! Where do these assumptions come from? Where do these snap opinions of others reside? In our previous experiences of course! Yet, notice how quickly our assumptions might change if these same drivers who cut us off in traffic, suffer from a cognitive impairment that affects their impulse control or judgment. Maybe we did not see the handicap placard hanging from the review mirror? Maybe because of their disability, they are operating a vehicle with hand controls in which, for a moment, their hands moved the wrong controls. Now what do we assume about them? What do we assume about ourselves?

Another reason we get tangled up in our assumptions is that we often cannot see the possibilities of what might lie beyond the moment. In other words, is there a greater lesson we can learn from by taking a step back and seeing the bigger picture? For example, there's a story in the Book of Exodus that recalls how the Israelites crossed the Red Sea (Exodus 14). According to the story, after releasing the Israelites from their slavery to the Egyptians, Yahweh leads them to edge of the Red Sea. Although elated with joy at their new found freedom, the people quickly assumed the worst when things didn't go as they planned:

> As Pharaoh approached, the Israelites looked up, and there were the Egyptians, marching after them. They were terrified and cried out to the LORD. They said to Moses, "Was it because there were no graves in Egypt that you brought us to the desert to die? What have you done to us by bringing us out of Egypt? Didn't we say to you in Egypt, 'Leave us alone; let us serve the Egyptians'? It would have been better for us to serve the Egyptians than to die in the desert!" Moses answered the people, "Do not be afraid. Stand firm and you will see the deliverance the LORD will bring you today. The Egyptians you

*see today you will never see again. The LORD will
fight for you; you need only to be still."*

*Then the LORD said to Moses, "Why are you crying
out to me? Tell the Israelites to move on. Raise
your staff and stretch out your hand over the sea
to divide the water so that the Israelites can go
through the sea on dry ground. I will harden the
hearts of the Egyptians so that they will go in after
them. And I will gain glory through Pharaoh and all
his army, through his chariots and his horsemen.
The Egyptians will know that I am the LORD when
I gain glory through Pharaoh, his chariots and his
horsemen." Then the angel of God, who had been
traveling in front of Israel's army, withdrew and
went behind them. The pillar of cloud also moved
from in front and stood behind them, coming
between the armies of Egypt and Israel. Throughout
the night the cloud brought darkness to the one side
and light to the other side; so neither went near the
other all night long. Then Moses stretched out his
hand over the sea, and all that night the LORD drove
the sea back with a strong east wind and turned
it into dry land. The waters were divided, and the
Israelites went through the sea on dry ground, with
a wall of water on their right and on their left.*

*The Egyptians pursued them, and all Pharaoh's
horses and chariots and horsemen followed them
into the sea. During the last watch of the night the
LORD looked down from the pillar of fire and cloud*

*at the Egyptian army and threw it into confusion.
He jammed the wheels of their chariots so that they
had difficulty driving. And the Egyptians said,
"Let's get away from the Israelites! The LORD is
fighting for them against Egypt." Then the LORD
said to Moses, "Stretch out your hand over the sea
so that the waters may flow back over the Egyptians
and their chariots and horsemen." Moses stretched
out his hand over the sea, and at daybreak the sea
went back to its place. The Egyptians were fleeing
toward it, and the LORD swept them into the sea. The
water flowed back and covered the chariots and
horsemen—the entire army of Pharaoh that had
followed the Israelites into the sea. Not one of them
survived. But the Israelites went through the sea
on dry ground, with a wall of water on their right
and on their left. That day the LORD saved Israel
from the hands of the Egyptians, and Israel saw the
Egyptians lying dead on the shore. And when the
Israelites saw the mighty hand of the LORD displayed
against the Egyptians, the people feared the LORD
and put their trust in him and in Moses his servant.*

So many assumptions were challenged that day. *Does God
really want us to go into the Sea? Did God bring us out to the
desert to die? Does God care about us?* The whole Exodus
experience which is told and retold each year at Passover,
teaches the Israelites and hopefully others, that God compels us
to always look at our times of physical, emotional and spiritual
deliverance with a new, life-giving perspective. As a result of

these and other stories, I am even more convinced that God loves to use irony in our lives. Irony is often God's way of getting our attention in order to grasp a deeper understand of ourselves, others and even our relationship with Him. For us today, the responsibility, then, is to let go of those old assumptions of how we have perceived our relationships and worldview up to that time. Perhaps this task involves examining what we want God to be for us, or how the world should work. Perhaps we need to rethink our unrealistic expectations of ourselves. By doing so, we just might be able to hear that still, small voice challenging us to embrace a more authentic, genuine and harmonious life. This is why Apostle Paul says, *"No longer conform to the pattern of this world, but be transformed by the renewing of your mind. . .then you will be able to discern what God's will is"* (Romans 12:2).

Indeed, one of the biggest difficulties people wrestle with is the loss of their assumptions. For example, if they're facing divorce or separation, there's the loss of the assumption that married people are supposed to live happily ever after. People are supposed to be rewarded and enjoy if they work hard and plan for the future. The problem is that there are no guarantees in life. This belief is also devastating when religious or spiritual assumptions are among the pieces on the ground.

Marie was such a person. A woman in her mid-forties, Marie was facing major changes in her life: She was not only going through menopause, but over the past year she had lost her husband, job and financial security. Her face told the story. Her appearance was disheveled. She wore no makeup and there were considerable dark circles under her eyes. She was clearly

74

overwhelmed with grief and depressed. I listened intently as she explained how she never thought her life would turn out this way. She always lived her life according to one, simple rule: *If you work hard and be a good person, you will have no regrets and fully appreciate what you have in the end.* The problem was that she felt betrayed because "life" did not keep its end of the bargain. She was having difficulty trying to reconcile being a good person who was filled with many regrets about how her life turned out. She lamented about missed opportunities, surrendered life-goals, and feeling unappreciated. Clearly her self-worth was attached to her "if, then" fail-safe rule of life (*If I work hard, then I will be rewarded*). She was prescribed a mild anti-depressant to take the edge off of her depression. In the following sessions, we continued to look at her story more closely, often noting the underlying assumptions tied to them. When a new assumption was uncovered, she wanted to blame herself for being "gullible." Eventually, she wanted to live a life with no assumptions; a lofty goal, but impossible to achieve. Furthermore, she wanted me to take away her assumptions. Again, this was not my responsibility. Her assumptions were hers' to own. I have mine. Finally, in getting her to reframe the question that was more solution-focused, she came to the insight that she had control over letting go (or at least modifying) which of those old assumptions no longer fit her life? Despite the fact that life may not have turned out the way Marie assumed and planned, she can still live a life with no regrets. In fact, she also found her daily empowerment as she was mindful to live each day with no regrets. *Why should I wait till the end of my life to look back on what I have been doing? I can do this each day!* Funny where we meet irony.

Janoff-Bulman (2002) notes that our assumptions are founded on our *beliefs* about life that we take for granted (or at least aware of), and therefore, are less likely to change. Beliefs such as *the world (people are) is benevolent, good, kind, etc. The world is meaningful, significant, etc. The self is worthy, valuable, precious, etc.* These assumptions do not necessarily need to be based on factual knowledge to be engrained in us, but may also include superstitions, perceptions, etc., that serve another purpose in our lives. For example, in my opinion, athletes are the most superstitious people in the world. Depending on the sport, athletes engage in all kinds of pre-game and game-time rituals in the hope that they will avoid errors, injuries and win the game. Some athletes maintain a bizarre diet, vowing only to eat certain foods before a game. Others make the sign of the cross to bless themselves before their turn or following scoring points. Still, others refuse to step on a boundary line going on or off a field, or they may even refuse to cut their hair or shave in order to keep a winning streak going. Does it work? Athletes seem to think so. In fact, what is evident to the spectator is that these rituals seems to focus the athlete for the task at hand, and thus making them feel in control in situations that may be out of their control. Perhaps the most familiar framework of assumptions is the law of causation: *If this and such happens, then this will happen.* However, all assumptions make us nearsighted to the potential of hidden blessings in the future, especially when we may not see the deeper lesson or benefit immediately.

The Lost Horse, a Chinese Folktale.

A man who lived on the northern frontier of China was skilled in interpreting events. One day, for no reason his horse ran away to the nomads across the border. Everyone tried to console him, but his father said, "What makes you so sure this isn't a blessing?" Some months later his horse returned, bringing a splendid nomad stallion. Everyone congratulated him, but his father said, "What makes you so sure this isn't a disaster?" Their household was richer by a fine horse, which his son loved to ride. One day he fell and broke his hip. Everyone tried to console him, but his father said, "What makes you so sure this isn't a blessing?"

A year later the nomads came in force across the border, and every able-bodied man took his bow and went into battle. The Chinese frontiersmen lost nine of every ten men. Only because the son was lame did the father and son survive to take care of each other. Truly, blessing turns to disaster, and disaster to blessing: the changes have no end, nor can the mystery be fathomed.

The Power of Mindful Learning

If there is one lesson this simple story teaches us is that we do not have everything in our lives (let alone the lives of others) figured out. Metaphorically speaking, we can be nearsighted when it comes to our lack of understanding the grand scheme of things. Just like the folktale, we assume that a certain misfortune will forever dictate our lot. We assume that God sees events exactly as we view them, and therefore, should operate by our set of rules. But truth be told, God's viewpoint transcends our time, space and egos. If we recall Job's story in the Bible, Job believed that he did nothing to *deserve* his suffering. As the story unfolds, it becomes clearer that Job's pain and sorrow were not the consequences of his actions. Yet, how many times when we experience emotional, physical or spiritual suffering do we often assume that we did something to bring it about? Sometimes we can point directly to the cause of our pain, as in the case of dropping a large stone on our foot, or experiencing the death of a loved-one, and other times we cannot. But in addition to examining our assumptions, we also must realize how we are governed by linear thinking, namely restricted to time, space and rational. These are the parameters we have learned to live by which have guided our assumptions and conclusions about who we are and the world in which we live. However, God is Spirit and is not limited to our time, space and logic, but instead, fills the void of all that has come before us and will come after. For example, God's love and wisdom is infinite and immeasurable. Ours' is but a dim glimpse of reality often dictated by conditions. Ironically, our perceptions work in a finite world, but when it comes to *seeking the Lord with all our heart, soul, mind and strength* (Mark 12:29-31), our assumptions and preconceived notions about God have to undergo a transformation as well. As a result, transformation is not a one-time phenomenon, but rather, it is a continuous work of God's Spirit in our lives. . .if we are open to it.

THE SUMMIT

Transformation in Mental Health

Transformation is all around us in the cycle of death and resurrection. Each year we witness this cycle evident in the change of seasons as Summer gives way to Autumn, which gives way to Winter, which gives way to Spring, etc. There is even a death-resurrection metaphor that underlines the work of psychotherapy. In fact more often than not, transformation occurs in the most unlikely ways when we are not paying attention. Years ago, in one of the mental health offices where I worked hung a framed quote from the family therapist Virginia Satir (1916-1988):

> *I want to love you without clutching,*
> *Appreciate you without judging*
> *Join you without invading,*
> *Invite you without demanding,*
> *Leave you without guilt,*
> *Criticize you without blaming,*
> *And help you without insulting.*
> *If I can have the same from you,*
> *Then we can truly meet each other.*

Day after day I passed by this quote, but never really stopped to *read* it, let alone, *understand* its impact on relationships both within and outside of counseling relationships. So one day eating my lunch I read and re-read that quote slowly. I remember thinking to myself, *"Powerful saying, but far too demanding. Too many conditions and changes would be required of people to reach this. Moreover, (I assumed) it's unrealistic to place this pressure on another person and expect them to keep their part of the bargain."* In counseling and pastoral settings, I have witnessed too many people, including myself, making excuses for not wanting to be authentic in relationships. *"I've been hurt, fool me once, shame on you, she hurt my feelings",* and so forth. And yet, there was something resonating within me, identifying with those words, as if I had truth staring me right in the face. For days and weeks that followed, this gnawing inside of me to reclaim my own authenticity only became stronger.

Satir's words pursued me like my shadow. Little did I realize that I was reading her goals for her own life. Born in 1916, Virginia Satir was certainly ahead of her time. Instead of viewing humanity's problems as stemming from the neurosis of her day, she believed problems were the result of how people were unprepared to cope with life's challenges; past, present, or future. She used to say, *"Life is not what it's supposed to be. It's what it is. The way you cope with it makes the difference."* Satir believed that all people are equipped with the capacity for growth, transformation, and continuing education; focusing her technique on finding a person's true inner self (1983). In fact, it could be said that Satir's life's passion in working with individuals and families was to empower them to live more congruent, genuine, lives.

Authenticity is often a foreign concept to many people. Yet despite not knowing what to call it, many people are attracted to genuineness and desperately want more of it in their relationships. But just how real can a person be with others? Because it's one thing to look in the mirror; it's another matter altogether not to succumb to the opinions of others. Too often we live our lives under the relentless bombardment of another person's condition for acceptance. Satir also used to say, *"We must not allow other person's limited perceptions to define us."* When you think about it we are raised with so many conditions placed on love and relationships, performance and perspectives, that we often approach life with a "what's the catch?" mentality. In his book, *The Return of the Prodigal Son,* Henri Nouwen paints a picture just how unfulfilling conditional love is:

> *At issue here is the question: "To whom do I belong? God or to the world?" Many of my daily preoccupations suggest that I belong more to the world than to God. A little criticism makes me angry, and a little rejection makes me depressed. A little praise raises my spirits, and a little success excites me. It takes very little to raise me up or thrust me down. Often I am like a small boat on the ocean, completely at the mercy of its waves. All the time and energy I spend in keeping some kind of balance and preventing myself from being tipped over and drowning shows that my life is mostly a struggle for survival: not a holy struggle, but an anxious struggle resulting from the mistaken idea that it is the world that defines me.*

> *As long as I keep running about asking: "Do you love me? Do you really love me?" I give all power to the voices of the world and put myself in bondage because the world is filled with "ifs." The world*

says: "Yes, I love you if you are good-looking, intelligent, and wealthy. I love you if you have a good education, a good job, and good connections. I love you if you produce much, sell much, and buy much." There are endless "ifs" hidden in the world's love. These "ifs" enslave me, since it is impossible to respond adequately to all of them. The world's love is and always will be conditional. As long as I keep looking for my true self in the world of conditional love, I will remain "hooked" to the world-trying, failing, and trying again. It is a world that fosters addictions because what it offers cannot satisfy the deepest craving of my heart.

In my work as a mental health therapist and pastoral professional, I assist people to become more authentic in their relationships, to take an honest look at themselves and consider what role and responsibility they have in relationships. Too often people want to blame others for their own mistakes, problems and sleepless nights. But if truth be told, according to the band The Eagles, *So often times it happens that we live our lives in chains, and we never even know we have the key* (lyrics from *Already Gone*). Again this philosophy sounds great, but it also takes great courage to turn the key, let alone, step out the chains and walk in one's new-found freedom. This is a similar metaphor found in Charles Dickens' *A Christmas Carol* (1843). Charles Dickens (1812-1870) was deeply disturbed by the way the poor were treated in his day. His writings were often viewed in response to the British government changing the welfare system known as the Poor Laws, requiring children to work in tin mines, factories and welfare applicants to work on treadmills, i.e., machine engine power turned by walking. In Dickens' eyes the Industrial Revolution drove many people into poverty, while at the same time, neglecting its obligation to provide humane social services. *A Christmas Carol*, is set on Christmas Eve in 1843, seven years after the death of Ebenezer Scrooge's business partner, Jacob Marley. To set the stage, Dickens' describes Scrooge as *"a squeezing, wrenching, grasping, scraping, clutching, covetous, old sinner!"* who finds no room in his heart for any form of kindness, compassion, love or generosity. In fact, he despises Christmas, deciding to spend it alone although he is invited to his nephew Fred's invitation. He even goes so far as to chase away two gentlemen who ask him for a donation to provide a Christmas dinner for the poor. That night, Scrooge is visited by Marley's ghost. Forced to wear the cumbersome chains of misery and regret in the afterlife, Marley warns Scrooge to change his greedy and unforgiving ways, otherwise he will experience the same miserable afterlife as himself. Scrooge is then visited by three additional ghosts – each in its turn, and each visit detailed in a separate stave – who accompany him to various scenes with the hope of achieving his transformation. By morning, Scrooge has undergone a complete transformation in his heart and soul. He breathes a sigh of relief as he realizes he has not missed Christmas, and begins to lavish goodwill and gifts on anyone he meets. Moreover, he cannot keep his new found joy to himself, especially to the Cratchit family. The lesson is well concluded: that there is hope for all of humanity because even the most *covetous old sinner* is capable of a change of heart. Yet, transformation occurs more than just on a spiritual level. It occurs on an emotional and psychological level too. Not only does the soul take a journey, but the psyche has to take one as well. Despite the various psychological foundational models (psychoanalytical, cognitive-behavioral, and humanistic-existential), that emphasize their own strengths and limitations, they all have a common thread; despite the psychological problem at hand, they all measure healing in terms of striving toward living a more authentic life (an experience best characterized by the act of finding oneself, then living in accordance with this self).

Moreover, by reclaiming authenticity, a person is much better positioned to move toward self-actualization and genuine satisfaction with life. Existentialist psychologist Rollo May states that this change *requires great courage to preserve inner freedom, to move on in one's inward journey into new realms* (1994). Authenticity allows one the ability to move past the preoccupation of things that are beyond one's control as well as to abandon unnecessary concerns over the preconceived notions of others with respect to oneself. In short, it is the ultimate form of empowerment and responsibility. Discovering our authentic selves, as well as the daily commitment to live congruently, we experience firsthand the personal freedom (and responsibility) it produces.

Following up on my analogy of climbing a mountain, many people also perceive mental health counseling and therapy similar to taking an inward journey of awareness and self-discovery. However, just as there are familiar themes of guides and fellow voyagers, a person's interior journey is not taken alone; the mental health therapist is also privileged to accompany the client into perhaps unfamiliar territory. For example, I have always compared the relationship between a therapist and client to that of Virgil and Dante in *The Inferno* (2013) by Alighieri. Considered to be Dante's (1265-1321) greatest literary work, *The Inferno* records a symbolic journey through Hell and is rich with the Christian themes of sin, salvation, and redemption: On the evening of Good Friday in 1300 AD, Dante writes that has lost his path through a dark wood and now wanders dreadfully through the forest. As the sun shines down on a mountain above him, Dante attempts to climb it but finds his way blocked by three beasts—a leopard, a lion, and a she-wolf. Terrified and stranded, Dante resigns himself to the dark wood and contemplates suicide. It is there he encounters the Roman poet Virgil, who tells Dante he has come to guide him back to his path to reach the mountain top. Virgil also adds that it was Beatrice, Dante's deceased beloved and two other holy women, who sent Virgil to guide him. But first, Virgil explains that their path will take them through Hell and that they will eventually reach Heaven, where his Beatrice waits. As they approach the gates of Hell, a sobering chill grips Dante (and the reader) as he takes note of the haunting inscription above. . . *Abandon All Hope, You Who Enter Here.* Perhaps this sign is a reminder that any inward journey is not without the danger of becoming overwhelmed at what one discovers to the point of despair.

From wanting to heal emotional and/or behavioral wounds, to simply wanting to feel better, people seek out mental health counseling in various inpatient and outpatient settings. It has been my experience that the majority of people come to counseling in a state of utter despair, believing that they have nowhere else to turn. Perhaps they are living in their own *dark wood of terror*, confronted by the demons of their past and don't know what else to do. Perhaps they may come to counseling holding out fragmented pieces of emotional, behavioral and/or spiritual brokenness, wondering how they can be made whole again? In this respect, the counseling process is like *The Inferno* as the therapist explores the depths of client's hell of addiction, abuse, traumatic experiences, etc. However unlike *The Inferno*, regardless of the emotional pain, suffering and woundedness, mental health therapists hold out hope, wisdom and redemption, as they agree to walk with their clients through this transformation toward living a more authentic life.

Interestingly, personal transformation in mental health has often been described in the language of "movement." From week to week, treatment goal progress is noted as clients typically move forward with insight, regress into familiar pain, or remain stuck or unchanged in their perspectives and behavioral patterns. Furthermore, when clients become increasingly aware of life-hindering, or even destructive, cognitive and/or behavioral patterns in their life, they are able to apply healthier choices and skills reflected in their perceptions and behavior both in and out of counseling sessions. A major contributor to a client's growth is a therapist's use of empathy and patience as the client's journey toward authenticity can be frightening due to the vast unknown. In his book, *On Becoming a Person,* psychotherapist Carl Rogers (1961) describes the irony of facing the unknown:

> *This book is about the suffering and hope, the anxiety and the satisfaction, with which each therapist's counseling room is filled. It is about the uniqueness of the relationship each therapist forms with each client, and equally about the common elements with which we discover in all these relationships. This book is about the highly personal experiences of each one of us. It is about a client in my office who sits there by the corner of the desk, struggling to be himself, yet deathly afraid of being himself—striving to see his experience as it is, wanting to be that experience and yet deathly fearful of the prospect.*

Although all classic and contemporary counseling theorists acknowledge a client's personal growth as an essential component to their theories, how these mental health professionals help people reclaim their authentic selves is achieved in different ways. For the most part, therapists are trained in various counseling theories that provide a framework for them to be a healing presence, understand the client's situation and intervene in helping their clients build life-giving skills. The theorists I have listed here are in no way exhaustive, but represent only a handful of paradigms I use in my practice to emphasize this journey toward my clients reclaiming authenticity.

Movement as coping: Karen Horney (1885-1952)

In the early days of psychoanalysis, "movement" in therapy was often described as a personal understanding of one's limitations and resolving unconscious conflicts, in order to integrate a healthier awareness of his/her strengths and growing edges, maturity, and development of the self (Yalom, 2009). Although *neurosis* is no longer a term used in the mental health field, Horney noted that *neurosis* often developed from basic feelings of anxiety, depression and irrational fears (1945). As a result, these feelings would then be projected onto others, whom a *neurotic* person believes is more intelligent and capable than himself/ herself. These initial observations led Horney to construct a paradigm based on how a person acts inauthentically by moving *toward, against,* or *away from* interpersonal relationships. Moreover, she asserted that as children in the early stages of human development, we learn four ways to protect ourselves from basic anxiety resulting from loneliness and helplessness:

- Securing love and affection by seeking attention and approval from others;
- Being submissive in overriding relationships;
- Attaining power by seeking prestige, achievement or admiration from others;
- Withdrawing by striving for self-sufficiency or perfection.

As we grow toward adulthood, Horney states that we develop coping strategies to guard against anxiety in terms of these interpersonal styles. For example, when *moving toward others*, people display compliance after admitting their own helplessness, and in-spite of their fears of rejection, attempts to gain affection of others and learn to depend on them. When *moving against others*, people experience relationships as hostile, and therefore, distrust the feelings and intentions of others toward themselves. When *moving away from others,* people largely become emotionally detached or disconnected from human affairs, creating an inner, isolated world for themselves. These people have a heightened need for privacy, independence, and self-sufficiency.

Movement Toward Others
A person accepts his/her own helplessness, and in-spite of his estrangement and fears tries to "win" the affection of others and to lean on them.

Movement Against Others
A person sees himself/herself as being powerful and superior. Seek to dominate others within relationships.

Movement Away From Others
A person largely becomes detached from human affairs, creating an inner, isolated world of themselves, heightened need for privacy, independence, and self-sufficiency. Can often appear to be aloof and unapproachable, and feel discomfort in most social situations.

91

The goal in counseling, then, is to recognize and heal from these maladaptive patterns of relating to others, while at the same time, work to transform these interpersonal relationships toward healthier, life-giving relationships. Once people become aware of how their irrational perceptions keep them from meeting their emotional, physical and even spiritual needs, the opportunity is there for them to realize that they too have such gifts to meet the needs of others in relationships. By reclaiming authenticity, people are more willing to see themselves as loving, generous, unselfish, sensitive, etc., thereby transforming these fears into friendlier, more loving and supportive relationships.

For example, Marcus, a 30-something male, suffers from severe depression and anxiety. A simple depression and anxiety scale confirmed his report. On his intake form he stated that he has struggled with self-esteem issues and relationships with women for as long as he could remember. On occasion, Marcus reported trying on-line dating, but said all his relationships ended up the same: After the first month in a relationship, his girlfriends "dumped him" without warning. Exploring this story further, Marcus recognized his continuous pattern of emotionally smothering his girlfriends because of his excessive fear of being rejected. At first, his girlfriends would love the attention, but quickly grew suspicious when his behavior escalated into a suffocating barrage of e-mails, texts, and Facebook entries. Admittedly, Marcus had a deep-seated fear of rejection, which was reinforced in his mind when his girlfriends would grow tired of his behavior and block his calls and texts. This perceived "rejection" would then spin Marcus into a state of depression, believing that he was "totally unlovable". Our overarching goals in counseling was clear: Be assessed for appropriate anti-depression and anti-anxiety medication, explore ways to heal from his fears of rejection, and then, transform these fears into being friendlier, more loving and authentic towards himself and others. The way we achieved these goals were two-fold: First, Marcus examined the way he set himself up for rejection in these relationships. His excessive neediness and fear of being alone was a driving factor. He took responsibility for his actions and ultimately looked at his own feelings toward loneliness in early childhood. Second, Marcus began to identify emotional and cognitive blocks that kept him from seeing himself as a loving, generous, sensitive person. In fact, his biggest obstacle to finding fulfillment in relationships was embracing himself as a person of value and worth. We took a closer look at him wanting to be authentic with himself, namely claiming his value, gifts and talents he possessed as a person, and then begin to embrace the risk and reward of being genuine to himself and others. . . regardless of who approves or not. These days, Marcus is still trying to find "Mrs. Right", but now his relationships are driven by healthier expressions of intimacy, and less by the fear and anxiety of being rejected.

Movement as stages of contact and growth: Fritz Perls

First articulated by Fritz Perls (1893-1970), Gestalt Therapy seeks to empower people toward reclaiming their authenticity by having them recognize their capacity to deal with their problems. In fact, Perls (1969) believed that because people know what problems they have, they are in the best position to use all of their abilities to solve them. Through awareness of their physical sensations, emotional responses, desires, and cognitive assumptions, people can be empowered by their choices about how they live their lives, especially how they engage with inter and intra-personal relationships. Therefore, it crucial that people realize "how" they are creating their lives in specific ways, over/ against "why" they came to be where they are in life. By focusing on the fragmented pieces of the inauthentic self, Perls, Hefferline and Goodman (1977) identified levels of potential transformation for people to begin integrating wholeness and balance in life:

Phony Stage
*People act in inauthentic ways as they
assume false roles out of ignorance
of who they really are*

Phobic Stage
*People feel vulnerable and helpless, and thus
hide their genuine selves to avoid rejection*

Impasse Stage
*People feel stuck and powerless, and
therefore, seek out help from others*

Implosive Stage
*People recognize their self-imposed limitations,
deal with unfinished business,*

and move toward greater integration
of fragmented pieces of the self

Explosive Stage

People experience reintegration and
wholeness, become authentic,
and able to feel and express emotions,
relationships are energized

In the *Phony Stage*, Perls assisted people in becoming aware of the roles they play to shield themselves from who they really are. By acting in inauthentic ways, people can therefore live according to society's barometer of approval instead of their own self-acceptance. Initially, Perls often received criticism for using the word "phony" to describe people, but according to him being phony meant to allow yourself to be defined by others' need for you to be something they want you to be for them. In fact, people often avoided being genuine because of their fears that they would not and could not measure up to the expectations of other. Usually stemming from unrealistic expectations experienced in childhood, people may have convinced themselves to not even bother being real, because the fear of being judged or rejected by another is too painful to risk the attempt.

The *Impasse Stage* is what I often see in clients who come for therapy. From my perspective, many people complain about being stuck in life. Some people describe themselves as having no energy and lifeless, feeling as though they are simply going through the motions at work, school, and family.

They portray themselves as if they cannot move beyond this fatalistic attitude, because somewhere in their lives, they have dropped a metaphorical anchor. Although they may expresses deep-seated desires to overcome great emotional and physical obstacles, people often struggle with the fear of change itself, as well as what that change then requires of them. The thought of leaving the familiar places in life, albeit painful and harmful, is too scary to explore. Consequently, a person might rather remain where they are emotionally, physically and/or spiritually instead of being faced with what they are unaccustomed to.

In the *Implosive Stage*, people recognize that in order to change they must be willing to acknowledge (and often grieve their losses) their choices in life, and be willing to embrace themselves anew. At this stage it is useful for people to recognize what they need to let go of, i.e., the former ways and perceptions that are no longer useful to them, in order to take on something more life-giving. For some people, taking on something better might include going back to school to complete or attain a new academic degree. Another life-giving example might include changing careers or putting more energy into neglected relationships. Whatever their decisions are, the key to this stage is for people to take responsibility for their perceptions and actions, as they begin to understand how they were living in non-congruent or disingenuous ways.

Finally, in the *Explosive Stage* people are now empowered to embrace a bright, new future. This awareness is time to be celebrated indeed! People are often amazed at the intensity of joy and freedom they have found. Ironically, they are also in disbelief at how inauthentic they had been living their lives for so long. They not only feel grateful for having a "veil lifted off their eyes", but also, are empowered to take responsibility for their actions with a new found sense of vitality and inner strength.

Randle, a CEO of a large corporation, was extremely introverted and socially inept person. He was in his mid-fifties, highly successful, and riddled with feelings of worthlessness. He had a history of alcohol abuse and an attempted suicide when he was 23 years old. He was raised to believe that hard work and success go hand in hand. Intertwined in this mentality was Randle's belief to never be satisfied with where you are in life, but always be striving for the next level. Growing up his parents and teachers always set the bar of acceptance and achievement high in order that he might "make something of himself one day." Needless to say, that motivation worked. What his family, friends, and competition saw on the outside was a man who was goal-oriented, sales-minded, and never willing to settle for second-best. The problem was that Randle's internal bar of acceptance kept moving further and further out of reach. He never took time to stop and enjoy the fruit of his labor, nor did he let anyone else. However, on the inside, Randle believed he never measured up in the business world. Furthermore, his family also suffered this belief. Since Randle was unwilling to settle for imperfection, his family lived as if they were always under the microscope of his definition of excellence. For example, in the business world, companies are known for offering "carrots and sticks", incentives and rewards, for those employees whose sales reach record proportions for the quarter or year. However, once the sales period closes, the bar of expectations of doing more for next time was always strictly endorsed. Randle affirmed this business practice not only with his employees, but also with his family. As a result, his family became emotionally distant toward Randle as they continuously felt as though they had to earn his acceptance and love.

Although Randle prided himself on achievement, his journey toward authenticity was a daunting task. We spent almost a year working on him coming to terms with who he was. By using a double-sided, hand-held mirror, Randle would spend the sessions looking at who he was. He would talk about his childhood, relationships growing up, and trying to live up to the expectations of others. At one point he identified himself as a "people-pleaser", always wanting to be the good boy by meeting the expectations of others, that is, once he knew what was required from him. In fact, this was a key issue for us to address in the therapist-client relationship. Once Randle exhausted identifying who he was in his past, I then asked him to flip the mirror over and visualize who he wanted to be. At first Randle was taken aback by the 5x magnification of this side of the mirror. In fact, he remarked how his image amplified his inner desire to be authentic. Apparently, this side of the mirror intensified more than just his wrinkles, dark circles and graying hair! All in all, Randle became quite good at distinguishing between the two sides of the mirror; the two sides of himself. Admittedly, this task was easy for Randle in the confines of the safe environment of therapy sessions; the challenging part was integrating the two into a reclaimed authentic self he felt secure enough to display in front of others. A core feature of being genuine for Randle was displaying compassion, hospitality and generosity. With the help of the 5x magnification side, once Randle was able to treat himself with compassion, being hospitable and generous towards others came effortless. His weekly homework assignments included practicing compassion, hospitality and generosity with himself and his family, who immediately noted that Randle was now speaking to them in softer tones. Over time, as Randle became more comfortable in his authentic skin, his compassion, hospitality and generosity became contagious in and around the agency to the point where his employees were now empowered to treat their coworkers alike.

Movement as motivation toward self-actualization: Abraham Maslow

A counseling model which most people are familiar with today is the Hierarchy of Needs Theory first proposed by Abraham Maslow in his 1943 paper *A Theory of Human Motivation.* Although the phrase and definition of "self-actualization" (the motivation to realize one's fullest potential) was first coined by neuropsychologist Kurt Goldstein (1878-1965), Maslow believed that self-actualizing people are basically curious by nature, and thus, seek personal fulfillment by expanding their knowledge of themselves and others. As a result, self-actualizing people appear to be fully engaged in any activity; guided by a larger set of values that stress goodness, beauty, and wholeness of life (Maslow, 2011). Often portrayed in the shape of a pyramid, Maslow understood humanity's most fundamental level of needs at the bottom. As people are able to satisfy their physical and emotional needs, they continued up the pyramid toward safety, love and acceptance, and eventually being totally fulfilled in life.

Maslow's Hierarchy of Needs

Self-Actualizing

Feeling and being empowered, enhanced creativity and problem-solving, sense of morality

↕

Esteem

Self-esteem, confidence, achievement, respect for others, respect by others

↕

Love/Belonging

Friendship, family intimacy

↕

Safety

Physical security, employment, resources, health, property

↕

Physiological

Food, water, sleep, rest, clothing, shelter

At the *Physiological level,* Maslow included the most basic needs that are vital to survival, such as the need for water, air, shelter, food, sleep, etc. He believed that these needs are the most basic and instinctive needs in the hierarchy because all needs become secondary until these physiological needs are met. Early on in my ministry I was working at a men's homeless shelter. I saw first-hand that once the men had their basic needs of food, clothing and shelter met, this empowered them to pursue employment and getting back on their feet financially. In fact, once these physiological needs were met on a daily basis, the majority of them started to set other goals for themselves. For some it was seeking employment. For others their goals were to be reunited with their estranged families, etc.

At the *Security level* Maslow noted that although one's safety and security needs are important for survival, they are just as demanding as the physiological needs. Examples of security needs include a desire for steady employment, health care, safe neighborhoods, and personal safety in the work environment.

When people reach the *Social level,* Maslow concluded that it was natural for people to recognize their need for belonging, love, and affection. Again, Maslow described these needs as less basic than physiological and security needs. However, relationships such as friendships, romantic attachments, and families help fulfill this need for companionship and acceptance, as well as involvement in one's social, community, or religious groups. After the first three levels have been satisfied, Maslow rationalized that self-esteem (*Esteem level)* becomes increasingly important. These include the need for relationships and accomplishments that reflect self-esteem such as personal worth, social recognition, and career goals to name a few. On the heels of getting one's esteem needs met, the next and highest level of Maslow's hierarchy can be reached, namely *Self-Actualization*. At this level, people are typically more self-aware, concerned with pursuits that lead toward personal growth, less concerned with the opinions of others, and interested in fulfilling their potential.

As previously mentioned, this pyramid model is very popular today because allows people to define for themselves what life goals would provide them a sense of self-fulfillment. Still, it is a misconception to conclude that Maslow's pyramid is a linear model where one level builds upon another. This belief is not necessarily the case. In fact, these developmental levels can be best understood in terms of their interrelatedness rather than disconnectedness of achievement. For example, in today's families there could be up to three, four and even five generations living under one roof. In families, churches and other community organizations, all of these generations are looking to have their emotional, physical and/or spiritual needs met. In all honesty, it is absurd to think that once people (at any generation) have met their physiological and security needs that they no longer are to be concerned about them. Instead, all of the Maslow's levels are given certain degrees of attention and focus at different times in our lives. The Johnson family represented this fact well. The Johnson's were your typical middle-class family who were struggling to squeeze a dollar out of forty cents to make ends meet. Although on the outside they seemed like any ordinary family raising two teenage daughters, their home life was a whirlwind of chaos and emotional turmoil. Ben, Mrs. Johnson's father, moved in with the family after his wife died five years ago. Ben receives a monthly income from his pension and social security, but also has been supplementing his income through dealing and using heroin on the side. His behavior clearly was the reason for chaos in the family. However, the Johnson's did not present this. Instead they decided to focus on tension that existed between their two teenage daughters: Cara was the model student; straight A's and popular, whereas Denise was viewed as the problem-child; failing grades, rebellious, multiple in-school detentions, etc. Although there were only 18 months that separated them in age, yet they could not be further apart in communicating and resentment.

The Johnson family contacted me after Ben was hospitalized for suffering a heart attack. At the urging of his cardiologist, Ben agreed to enter rehab. In fact, Ben had no choice. According to his doctor, Ben would not survive another heart attack let alone, make it another six months if he continued in his addiction. While Ben was in rehab, the rest of the Johnson family and I identified the roles families play when there is an addicted person. Dad, mom, Cara and Denise were surprised to understand how one family member's addiction controls other family members. As a result, they came to understand how the roles families play (enabler, hero, lost person, etc.) are understood as a means of coping with disorder and chaos ensued by the addicted family member.

Eventually guilt and blame directed at the sibling rivalry was healed through understanding and forgiveness. When they all were in a healthier place (including Ben), I helped them identify what goals they wanted for themselves and as a family. By using Maslow's Hierarchy of Needs, each member was able to identify what level they were in. They even began identifying ways they could help each other attain their goals. For families, understanding how Maslow's Hierarchy of Needs are fluid, not linear, empowers them to perceive events as neither positive or negative, but rather identifies how they will respond in terms of being authentic toward one another.

Movement as client-centered positive self-regard: Carl Rogers

Similar to Maslow's *Theory of Human Motivation*, Rogers' *Client-Centered Theory* took the concept of reclaiming authenticity toward personal fulfillment one step further. Similar to Perls, Rogers believed that all people have an inherent sense of value, dignity and worth. As a result, people basically know what is best for them to not only survive but also thrive in life. Unfortunately, there are times when people get off track and do not live according to their authentic goals and thus, they fail to thrive. Therefore, Rogers' main goal in counseling was to help people reclaim their authentic selves, as he himself modeled respect for them and their beliefs, unconditional positive regard, and being genuine and as authentic as he can in the therapeutic search (Rogers, 1951). For example,

This book is about me, as I sit there with that client, facing him, participating in that struggle as deeply and sensitively as I am able. It is about me as I try to perceive his experience and the meaning and the feeling and the taste and the flavor that it has for him. It is about me as I bemoan my very human fallibility in understanding that client, and the occasional failures to see life as it appears to him, failures which fall like heavy objects across the intricate, delicate web of growth that is taking place. It is about me as I rejoice at the privilege of being a midwife to a new personality—as I stand by with awe at the emergence of a self, a person as I see a birth process in which I have had an important and facilitating part (page 6).

A common misperception about Roger's *Client-Centered Theory* was that he was all about presence and congruence, and not much on demonstrating technique. In fact, I believe that Rogers' life-affirming presence was his technique. Using the metaphor of how creeks flow into rivers, which flow into oceans, Rogers developed a set of stages that captured the flow toward authenticity. Personal growth was therefore characterized by a person's movement from his/her *internal rigidity* towards increased *internal fluidity*, a deepening sense of self and one's internal life. Once a person developed a sense of awareness and acceptance of his/her own feelings, moving toward an *external fluidity* with the world, other people, and oneself involve became less threatening (Rogers, 1985).

Stage One: People are willing to communicate anything about themselves

- To what extent are you able to talk about yourself, versus having a preference for communicating about externals?
- To what extent do you spend time considering what is going on inside yourself?
- To what extent are you comfortable with ambiguity?
- In what ways do you manage and cope with ambiguity?

Stage Two: People discuss only external events and other people

- To what extent do you consider how you feel about people, things, events and circumstances? (Be careful to consider feelings (emotions) rather than thoughts / prejudices / beliefs.)
- To what extent do you prefer circumstances to be one thing or the other?
- To what extent do you comfortably own personal responsibility, versus perceiving problems as external to yourself? (Be careful to avoid equating personal responsibility with blame.)

Stage Three: People begin to talk about themselves, but only as an object

- To what extent do you talk (about yourself) in the first person ("I"), versus speaking in the second person ("You"; e.g. "If your career is important to you then you make the personal sacrifices required."), or speaking in the third person ("One", "People", "Everyone"; e.g. "One does what one can."; "People love a bit of gossip.")?

- To what extent are you aware of what you are feeling now (in real time), rather than focusing on only feelings you have felt in the past?
- How comfortable are you talking about what you are feeling now (in real time), rather than talking only about feelings you have felt in the past?

Stage Four: People discuss strong emotions that they have felt in the past

- To what extent are you typically willing to bring into your awareness what you are feeling right now?
- When you are aware of what you are feeling right now, how willing are you to:
- Acknowledge to yourself your own mild/convenient feelings?
- Acknowledge to yourself your own intense/inconvenient feelings?
- Talk about a) and/or b) with a trusted person?
- Put your feelings into action (e.g. to cry if you feel very sad; to rage if you feel anger; to embrace if you feel love)?
- To what extent are you typically aware of inconsistencies and contradictions within yourself?
- How willing are you to talk about such inconsistencies and contradictions within yourself?

- How enthusiastic are you about addressing inconsistencies and contradictions within yourself?
- How much of a risk is it for you to share something of yourself in a new close relationship?

Stage Five: People begin the express present feelings

- How eager are you to embrace an awareness that what you feel, however unacceptable, is, at least in part, who you really are?
- How enthusiastic are you to approach in yourself what you do not know about yourself, with the attendant risk that you might like / dislike what you discover?
- How eager are you to achieve precision in your understanding and description regarding how you feel / are feeling?
- To what extent do you engage in an internal dialogue (words and/or images) when faced with internal contradictions and inconsistencies?

Stage Six: People now allow previously denied or distorted experiences into their awareness

- To what extent can you allow yourself fully to be yourself, to feel and experience without reservation, while at the same time recognizing what is taking place?
- To what extent are you aware of the processes that underlie your surface responses – your own deeply-held values and motivations?

- How eager are you to suppress your own tears, sighs and chuckles, unless convenient?

Stage Seven: People experience irreversible change and growth

- To what extent are you able to recognize the culmination of the processes that have been taking place from Stage One, and also the final and complete loosening of their rigidness.

Movement as social interest: Alfred Adler

A contemporary of Sigmund Freud, physician and psychotherapist Alfred Adler (1870-1937) believed that humans are social beings and that our most basic goal is to find our sense of authenticity in relationships. Although heredity and environment factors might also have strong influences on our perceptions, decisions and behaviors, Adler believed that we are capable of making our own choices, and therefore, we move in the directions of our life goals.

Adler's life work focused more on people's emotional and physical health and well-being rather than their pathology. In fact, he often educated people about overcoming the limitations of them in service to society (*gemeinschaftsgefhle*), instead of striving toward individual superiority and compensation (*ichgebundenheit*). In other words, authentic people should neither lose themselves in their grandiose fictions, nor live vicariously through others. Instead, their deepest desires are to integrate their personal goals into activities that improve family and community (Sweeney, 2009). For example, as a child Adler overcame numerous physical illnesses and often received encouragement to strive toward excellence in school from his father. Through these early experiences, Adler developed his understanding of the *inferior complex*, namely, that all human beings have the potential to overcome physical and emotional (inferiority or inadequacy) limitations and attain authenticity through superiority or personal fulfillment. However, Adler cautioned this process of striving from inferiority to superiority was not to develop an arrogant, selfish, or condescending manner or attitude toward others. Instead, in developing personal and social skills, people are encouraged to also assist others in achieving similar goals and realize their potential and abilities. In other words, by helping others we are helping ourselves, and vice versa. We might even say that since we strive to reclaim our authenticity, we are compelled to help others reclaim theirs. Furthermore, our goals define a healthy sense of losing ourselves and finding ourselves by a willingness to develop ourselves fully and *contribute* to the welfare of others (Adler, 2009). Indeed, self-love and other-love develop together and support one another. For example, there is an amusing story about a nun who wanted to learn how to water ski. She had never water-skied before, but always had the desire. So in her spare time, she took lessons, but no matter how hard she tried, she never learned how to balance herself on her water skies. As a result, she never mastered the art of water skiing. However, her attempt of trying something new empowered her to explore other untapped areas of her religious and spiritual life that enhanced her quality of service toward others.

In a counseling setting, the role of the Adlerian therapist is to be a co-worker with people to not only examine their values, feelings of inadequacy or inferiority, personal assumptions, and misperceptions, but also, to encourage them toward a more useful, authentic way of living for themselves and others in community. Therefore, transformation from individual to societal concerns is a life-long process of mutual integration (albeit in identifiable stages) that benefits all of humanity:

Empathy and Relationship Stage:

- Therapist and clients strive to establish an empathic, cooperative, working relationship. The therapist models hope, reassurance, and encouragement to clients in this initial, unfamiliar stage.

Information Stage:

- Therapist gathers relevant information from the client, namely the details of the presenting problem and overview of general functioning. The therapist explores the client's early childhood situation, memories, and dreams that have shaped perceptions of self, others, and the world at large.

Clarification Stage:

- Therapist helps the client clarify any vague thinking with questions designed to identify consequences of his/her ideas and behavior. For instance, what perceptions does the client have about himself/herself and others which need to be simplified in order to be understood?

Encouragement Stage:

- Therapist encourages the client to see the risks and rewards of thinking and behaving in a new direction; to move in a new direction, away from behaviors and assumptions that are no longer life-giving. The therapist also helps client clarify feelings about his/her efforts and results.

Interpretation and Recognition Stage:

- Therapist interprets the client's feelings of inferiority and the possibilities of reclaiming authenticity toward feelings of superiority. To facilitate this stage, the client identifies what has previously been avoided in his/her development, and integrates a new found awareness of how his/her birth order, earliest recollections and dreams have contributed to his/her perceptions.

Knowing Stage:

- Therapist reinforces the client's self-awareness of his/her life and feelings about potential successes. In this stage, the client knows what needs to be done but may feel blocked. Further encouragement and assurance from the therapist is needed.

Emotional Breakthrough Stage:

- When needed, the therapist promotes emotional breakthroughs with "missing experiences" that correct past or present negative influences. Because the client may feel blocked from the previous stage, he/she may be unable to see the larger context of positive experiences helped shape perspectives too. To achieve this awareness, the therapist may also use role-playing, guided imagery, and group dynamics to assist in this process.

Doing Differently Stage:

- Therapist encourages client to convert new insights into a more authentic attitudes and begins to experiment with comparing new and old behavior.

Reinforcement Stage:

- The therapist encourages client toward significant changes by affirming positive results and feelings, and evaluating progress.

Social Interest Stage:

- Therapist uses client's newly discovered feelings to extend cooperation and caring about other people. Client is encouraged to give generously of himself/ herself and to take necessary risks in order to awaken feelings of equality among peers.

Goal Redirection Stage:

- Therapist challenges client to let go of the former inauthentic self by dissolving the old way of life and adopting new values.

Support and Launching Stage:

- Therapist and client celebrate launching into a new, creative, and gratifying way of living for him/her and others. Client embraces a path of continual growth for self and others.

Larry was a semi-retired chemist who had a wealth of beautiful memories of a loving wife, raising children, fulfilling career, and family vacations. However, he noticed that over time he was not as content as he used to be. His children were grown and raising a family of their own. He and his wife were feeling the physical and emotional effects of older adulthood, and his spiritual life was a little "sluggish." In spite of everything, Larry felt as though his best days were behind him. I begged to differ. We talked at length about his life; past, present and future. We talked about his struggles to raise a family and feel secure in his career. We talked about his hopes and dreams for his children and grandchildren. But most of all, we talked about Larry's generativity, a developmental stage in an older adult's life where a person expresses concern for the next generation (Erikson, 1998). Coined by developmental psychoanalyst Erik Erikson, generativity is often expressed in various ways, from stopping and healing the cycle of physical, emotional, and sexual abuse, to passing on family traditions or improving the water and vegetation conditions in one's community. In other words, a person strives to make a difference with his/her life by improving the lives of future generations. Perhaps what is striking about generativity is that every culture has its own expression of giving back to its generations, even generations that have yet to be born. For Larry we explored ways he could be pro-active in his giving back to his family, friends and community. Because of Larry's chemistry background he began working alongside some local farmers to study the effects of bio-chemical reactions related to plant and animal growth. He also helped them make better selections regarding specific chemical products developed to assist in the production of food, feed, and fiber include herbicides, fungicides, insecticides, plant growth regulators, fertilizers, and animal feed supplements. He has even begun to dabble a bit in his own backyard organic farming. These days Larry is busier than ever and his physical and emotional stamina is remarkable. Oh and by the way, Larry's spiritual life has blossomed into a new found gratitude as he likens his relationship with God to that of farmer; one who sows seeds of grace, peace, and hope in others for a future harvest of love and joy.

All in all, it has been my experience that if people develop a social interest at the personal level, they are more likely to feel a deeper belonging or connectedness to humanity, and therefore, are more able to empathize with their fellow human beings. Once this perspective is understood, the task of reclaiming our authenticity is not so daunting. Nevertheless, reclaiming the parts of ourselves that have been stolen, lost or given away should be attempted in what is manageable for us each day, regardless of how immense the mountain is before us. In fact, the old saying is true: each of us has a way of *making mountains out of mole-hills*. Or if you prefer William Shakespeare's phrase, *much ado about nothing*, either way you say it, we tend to make our problems, situations and personal growth more difficult than what they are, or need to be.

When Mountains Become Obstacles

In the book, *Mountains Beyond Mountains* (2003), Harvard professor and medical doctor Paul Farmer uses his skills of contemporary medicine to serve Haiti's most vulnerable. Ironically, it is in the mountains of Haiti where he encounters the on-going spread of communicable diseases, namely HIV and tuberculosis, with little to no medicine. Through his medical and political efforts, Farmer brought hope to those who live in despair by supplying medicine to improve their lives. Interestingly, his story is set against the background of a Haitian proverb, *beyond mountains there are mountains.* Loose translation: It seems as though once you solve one problem, another problem arises, and so forth.

Being on a psycho-spiritual journey toward reclaiming our authenticity doesn't necessarily guarantee us avoiding the obstacles of emerging mountains, or one problem after another. In fact if anything, a psycho-spiritual journey makes us even more aware of the mountains in our lives. This awareness I believe is a gift from God that produces a kind of lived-wisdom that enables us to climb with perseverance, endurance and even patience. A word of caution here: Just because we have successfully scaled one mountain in life does not mean we have scaled them all. Each mountain has its own distinct ancient wisdom and challenges we need to hear and integrate into our lives, especially once we have reach its summit.

A Spiritual Crisis: Drawing Close to God

I have yet to meet anyone who has not, at one time or another, questioned the existence and/or the actions of God, struggled with their faith, searched to find peace during emotional and physical storms, or even grappled with finding answers to life's traumatic questions of suffering and death. I encounter these and other issues in people (and myself) most of the time. Regardless of the issue, some people rationalize their circumstances by simply dismissing a difficult issue, give up the struggle, throw up their hands, and consider everything as meaningless, pointless, and beyond their understanding. Such people often join the chorus of Frederich Neitchze or Albert Camus, declaring that God must be dead, or at least wants to be left alone. Then there are others who are much less dissuaded that God cannot be known, let alone experienced. In fact, some people regardless of circumstances are even more motivated to pursue their spiritual path in the midst of emotional, physical or spiritual dilemmas. This determination is almost as if an inaudible brushstroke of God's breath has sparked a relentless pursuit of knowing who this divine being is. Even if people do not know what has happened to them once they encountered God, they know they are never going to be the same.

The Soul Takes a Journey Too!

Transformation in the spheres of mental health and spirituality should not be limited to a purely psychological endeavor. In fact, a few in society attempt to educated the masses into believing that the empirical, scientific method, of knowing God is the only verifiable means. In other words, the only way of proving the legitimacy of a person's relationship or experience with God is to only be confirmed by quantitative, measurable data. Moreover, the subjective topic of spirituality is therefore often ridiculed or dismissed by science since it does not so neatly fit into these criteria. Nevertheless, there are legitimate ways to measure spirituality's effects on how people live out the awakening of their souls. The key to this endeavor is that in reclaiming our authenticity we must realize that our soul also has a journey to make in terms of finding peace, satisfaction, even its home in an inauthentic world. For example, thirteenth century theologian and scholar Bonaventure notes that the word for 'journey' in the Latin term is *itinerarium*, which means an itinerary or plan, a journey in general, or making a pilgrimage to the Holy Land. What is important to note is that *'itinerarium'* expresses an action, a plan, or a prayer of our heart, soul and mind searching for God. Thus Bonaventure emphasizes that no person can be happy unless he/she transcends, or rises above their own self-interests. Furthermore, transcendence is only possible with God's help which is available to all who seek it from their hearts in fervent prayer (Cousins, 1978), and flows unforced from a desire to see others experience the same.

As previously mentioned, drawing close to God, even having the desire to draw close to God, is risky. It is risky because perhaps we fear that we might discover that we do not have God all figured out. At first blush, God just might not be for us who we want God to be (or behave) for us. We think we know God but we do not. We *assume* things to be a certain way but in the end when we call upon the Lord, as I always say. . . *"get ready. . .strap yourself in. . .and hold on tight!"* Having the courage to know God beyond the limits of our senses shatters whatever man-made box we have put God in. In fact, as we are reclaiming our authenticity this shattering of our preconceived ideas of God is inevitable. The mind, and yes sometimes our entire being, undergoes a shattering in every conceived form because these perceptions only represent a very, very, very limited understanding of who God really is. In fact, our human language more often than not greatly limits our ability to explain what God has touched in us.

Personally, I do not believe God shows up in our lives by accident. In fact, just as God loves the use of irony, so too does God love to show up in the ordinariness of our lives (Wicks, 1995). When we are not used to seeing the hand of God in our lives, we marvel at the times when God becomes visible through what we would refer to as the miraculous. Throughout the centuries mystics (John of the Cross, Meister Eckhart, Teresa of Avila, Jalaluddin Rumi, Francis of Assisi, Padre Pio, to name a few) were people who possessed such an unfathomable desire to have total connection or union with God, that they were accustomed to seeing and hearing God in all aspects of their lives. To them, miracles were the standard, not the exception. Seeing the divine extraordinarily in the human ordinary was commonplace, and yet, they were often tormented by their own emotional, physical and spiritual demons (Bodo, 2007). Nevertheless, divine insights and wisdom, visions, healings, vivid dreams, encounters with angels or other beings, ecstatic altered states of consciousness, etc., were so "out of the ordinary", that such experiences (and the mystics themselves) were sometimes viewed with suspicion and fear by established religions. Yet despite such resistance, these divine experiences carried with them messages of hope, deliverance, reform, and peace for all generations; times when God was about to do something new that had never been experienced before. Old assumptions and ecclesiastical structures simply could not contain what the Spirit was doing in the lives of others. Although attempts were often made to discredit either the mystic or the mystical experience itself, the transformation that occurred in both the mystic and others who *had eyes to see and ears to hear,* was undeniable. Physiological changes in prolonged mystical states are quite common such as: decreased breathing, shallow pulse, decreased circulation and brain waves, and lack of awareness of the body. In such a state of "rapture" described by Christian and non-Christian mystics, the body seems to be on the verge of dying.

For example, Teresa of Avila (1515-1582) experienced periods of intense sickness and spiritual ecstasy most of her life. Sometimes she confronted the awful terror of sin and her inadequacy of dealing with it, while other times she had comforting visions of Christ and angels. In one such vision, Teresa experienced an angel piercing her side with a flaming sword:

> *In his hands, I saw a golden spear, with an iron tip at the end that appeared to be on fire. He plunged it into my heart several times, all the way to my entrails. When he drew it out, he seemed to draw them out, as well, leaving me all on fire with love for God. . .The pain was so strong that it made me moan several times, and yet the sweetness of the pain was so surpassing that I couldn't possibly wish to be rid of it. My soul couldn't be content with anything but God. It wasn't a physical pain, but a spiritual one, even though my body did feel it considerably. This pain lasted many days, and during that time, I didn't*

want to see to anyone, but only to cherish my pain,
which gave me a greater bliss than any created
things could give me.

(Medwick, 1999)

As a result of this ecstatic experience Teresa believed that the pure love the angel injected into her heart, opened up her mind to have a deeper perspective of the God's love for the humanity. In fact, Teresa wrote in *The Interior Castle* that while in this rapturous state, the soul *"is utterly dead to the things of the world, and lives solely in God...I do not know whether in this state she has enough life left to breathe. It seems to me she has not; or at least that if she does breathe, she is unaware of it."*

For too long now, certain aspects of healthcare, mental health, religious establishments and society have misunderstood the significance of such mystical religious/spiritual experiences. Since the Age of Enlightenment (18th century), religious and spiritual experiences have been held as suspect by a few in society who attempt to provide some rational-philosophical explanation as to when, where, why, and how a divine being transcends the unfathomable profundity of heaven and reach into our lives? As a mental health researcher I understand the need to provide empirical evidence for improving a person's mental health. In fact, because mystical religious/spiritual experiences are so subjective, trying to measure its influence is like attempting to nail Jello® to the wall. Still, we can understand the relevance of such experiences when we look at the end result, namely, *how is a person's life transformed by such experiences? Is it leading him/her in life-giving ways? How is the person's interpersonal and intrapersonal relationships affected? In what ways is the person feeling closer to or alienated from God?*

Within every generation, there is a remnant of people who continue to experience God in unique and dynamic ways that turn them and their communities upside down, inside out, and every which way imaginable, spiritually speaking. From a sociological point of view, every religion within its culture expresses a unique perspective through people's beliefs and rituals responding to how the Transcendent Being touches their souls. In fact, there is great value to understanding these beliefs and behaviors in their subjective context, as well as understand the outcome or benefit they have on people and their society at large.

The fourth and fifth editions of the *Diagnostic and Statistical Manual of Mental Disorders,* list various religious and spiritual experiences associated with disturbing or distressing mental health issues. Examples included upsetting experiences that involve loss or questioning of faith, problems associated with conversion to a new faith, or questioning of spiritual values that may not necessarily be related to an organized church or religious institution (For a more thorough account of religious/ spiritual problems I invite you to explore Dr. David Lukoff's work in this area). Such religious and spiritual experiences include:

Mystical experiences
New Religious Movements and Cults
Psychic Openings
Visionary Experiences
Kundalini Awakening
Near-Death Experience
Possession Experience
Shamanic Crisis
Loss of Faith
Alien Encounters
Terminal & Life-Threatening Illness
Changes in Membership, Practices & Beliefs

At first blush we might raise the question, *"If religion and spirituality are meant to be up-lifting, beneficial to our overall well-being (and society at large), what problems might possible arise when we directly encounter God or the divine?"* Admittedly, spiritual emergencies and crises often occur when religious/spiritual changes become chaotic and overwhelming to the person. In his reprinted book *A Magician Among the Spirits* (2004), Harry Houdini (1874-1926) devoted most of his non-professional life exposing fraudulent "spiritualists" of his day (*Boston Medium Margery, the Davenport Brothers, Annie Eva Fay, the Fox Sisters, the Daniel Dunglas Home, Eusapia Pallandino*). Being a firm believer in God and the afterlife, Houdini sought authenticity in people's claims that they experienced God first hand. He often looked for confirmation and genuineness that he too sought following his wife's death.

For me, whether it is in a pastoral or mental health setting, it is not my intention to question the validity of such experiences. By this I mean that the focus of a spiritual/clinical attention, and the distress or impairment that follows for people, may be real or it may have been imagined. Nevertheless, in listening to a person's full story we are able to find the nuggets of truth, as well as positive and negative after-effects such experiences have on people's lives. Unfortunately, history is tainted with stories of how some people try to force or imitate a mystical religious/spiritual experience artificially through illicit drugs, oxygen deprivation, etc. In this context something mysterious may occur, such as seeing bright lights, hearing voices, chills, or other psychosomatic means. However, once this altered experience has concluded, many do not typically feel a personal transformation in their perceptions, attitudes and behaviors has occurred. Life will more than likely go on same as it ever was, and they might feel no deeper devotion to God or a more profound purpose in life.

20th century American philosopher and psychologist William James (2013) describes the characteristics of mystical experiences in his well-known collection of lectures in *The Varieties of Religious Experience.* In lectures 16 and 17 James states that there are four characteristics that all mystical experiences have in common:

- *Ineffability*- an experience that defies expression, i.e., attempting to describe an experience beyond mere words.

- *Noetic Quality* – an experience of insight into depths of truth unknown before. They contain illuminations, revelations and are full of significance that remain a personal witness for some time.
- *Transiency* – a mystical state, albeit powerful and dramatic, cannot be sustained for long periods of time.
- *Passivity* – an experience when a person feels as if his/her own will were grasped and held by a superior power

What I have discovered in dealing with people's stories regarding their first-hand encounters with God, is that what separates a genuine religious/spiritual experience from an artificial one is the transformation, or results, that occurs in them, or not. Some of my questions include:

- *What do you notice about yourself that you were not aware of before?*
- *What does this experience mean for you?*
- *To what degree do you feel your life has changed? 60, 120, 180, 360 degrees?*
- *Where is the experience challenging you in your life?*
- *Who are the people in your life that have noticed a changed?*
- *Who might benefit from your experience? Who might be burdened?*
- *What new calling or direction in your life do you now sense?*
- *What questions remain for you?*

For people who have experienced a genuine mystical religious/spiritual encounter with God, they are never the same. Their values and goals have undergone a life transformation from being singular and selfish, to other-centered (and God centered) and benevolent. In addition to this change, people may often struggle with trying to make sense of their encounters with God. A note of caution: These life-long changes do not occur overnight; they may take several years for people to integrate them in their lives. For example, a near-death experience (NDE) is defined as a profound psychological event that may occur to a person close to death or, if not near death, in a situation of physical or emotional crisis (Greyson, 2000). Because it includes transcendental and mystical elements, an NDE is a powerful event of consciousness; it is not mental illness. Whether happening "truly near death" or under benign circumstances, the NDE contains powerful images and emotions, usually of peace and love though sometimes terror, despair, guilt. An NDE may include an out-of-body experience and vivid perceptions of movement, light or darkness; encounters with deceased loved ones, unfamiliar entities and/or spiritual presences; sometimes a life review, a landscape, a sense of overpowering knowledge and purpose (Ibid, 2000).

Stoudt, Jacquin, and Atwater (2006) note that it takes an average of 12.7 years for people to emotionally, physically, psychologically, and/or spiritually adjust to a near death experience; the longest recorded being 42 years. In fact, during this time that have identified six challenges people encounter when integrating their NDE:

- *Processing a Radical Shift in Reality*- People experience a radically new concept of life, death, the afterlife, body, mind, and spirit.

- *Accepting the Return*—People are sent back from what is often described as "heavenly", a place of unconditional love and light. As a result, people who experience this no longer fear death, but express a "yearning" or a feeling; a homesickness for the environment they experienced during their NDE.

- *Sharing the Experience*—People feel as though they need to share their experience, not just to be loved and accepted, but also to help process and understand what happened. Although at times they lack the words to describe the vividness of their NDE, they also express frustration in choosing confidants who would not dismiss or pathologize what they encountered. At times, divorce and/or career changes have occurred.

- *Integrating New Spiritual Values With Earthly Expectations*—People express emotional and sometimes physical pain, in restructuring their lives, namely putting the pieces back together that may no longer fit in terms of perspectives, relationships, and assumptions. Many expressed the need to tell others to be more loving and forgiving in their relationships. Sometimes integrating the NDE causes friction in other areas of people's lives in terms of religion, politics, careers, financial resources, and spirituality.

- *Adjusting to Heightened Sensitivities and Supernatural Gifts*—People often experienced a major shift in their sensitivity toward vibrational energy, such as strong emotions, negative energy, being acutely aware of odors, visions, tastes, sounds and touch. Some expressed sensitivity being around technology (wearing watches, computers, etc.), and often would have a heightened sense of intuition (telepathy, seeing auras, communicating with animals, etc.).

- *Finding and Living One's Purpose*—People often struggle with the reason why they were sent back to the earthly realm, and they often spend the rest of the lives discovering and fulfilling that purpose. Some believed that they were sent back to serve and teach others about loving unconditionally, being more tolerant toward themselves and others, and help others lead more authentic, spiritually rewarding lives.

As I listen to these extraordinary stories about people who encounter God via a near-death experience or experience God in everyday, ordinary ways, a key component that helps people process any type of supernatural encounter is loss and grief. Most people are familiar with the pain and grief we experience when a loved-one dies (physical, emotional or spiritual). We have lost a person whom we have loved, and perhaps been loved by. We grieve the emotional, physical and even spiritual bonds we have shared that have been severed by the finiteness of humanness. However, grief is not limited to a physical death, for whenever we experience change in our lives, albeit positive and celebratory, we also experience a degree of separation and loss from what was once familiar. The result is a grief reaction on some personal level. Jeffreys (2011) makes this concept even easier to remember: Change = Loss = Grief. Changes in our lives should not be viewed as necessarily a negative thing. In fact, some changes are for the better: Bar Mitzvahs, confirmations, marriages, a new job, moving closer to family, even having surgery to correct an illness or stave off a spreading disease. All these life experiences have elements of both sorrowful loss and hopeful expectations in them. While we often think of events like a high-school or college graduation ceremony as marking an ending, it's not. Instead, commencement, as the name implies, also marks a beginning. This beginning can be understood as turning a new page in our lives with new opportunities, while at the same time letting go of the familiar routines and surroundings. Unfortunately, tension accompanies many life-changing events, because we have a deep desire to remain with and enjoy the familiar. Nevertheless, when we experience profound religious, spiritual and mystical states, we often awaken to the fact that there is someone and something beyond ourselves; greater than ourselves. In the grand scheme of things, we understand how finite and earth-bound we are, when compared to the greater expanse of the earth, universe, and beyond. Still this awareness should not immobilize us but rather empower us toward authenticity to make a difference in the lives of others and humanity where we live.

Author David Mitchell (2004) poses the thought that *"our lives amount to no more than one drop in a limitless ocean. . .yet what is an ocean, but a multitude of drops?"* In his novel, *Cloud Atlas,* Mitchell portrays humanity's nature as being fixed in victimization, i.e., the way individuals prey on one another, groups on groups, nations on nations, tribes on tribes. And yet in this backdrop of fatalism, one person is reshaped from a killer into a hero, and a single act of kindness ripples across centuries that inspire others in the future. Therefore, could it not also be said that a single act of cruelty also ripples across centuries as well? Indeed. However, this does not mean that we cannot make a difference in their lives of others. For example, Loren Eiseley's *The Star Thrower* (1969) has be told and retold in many versions by countless people. It is a motivational story that depicts the impact one little girl's actions has on a beach full of starfish. After a night of storms, hundreds of starfish were washed up on the beach. As she walked along the shore, she noticed several starfish were still alive and she began to throw them back into the ocean. This behavior went on for quite some time, all of which was being watched from afar by an inquisitive tourist. When curiosity got the better of him, he joined her on the beach and asked her if she believed she was wasting her time? Did she really think her actions made any difference? After all, with so many dead starfish what effect could she possibly have that day? With a smile on her face, she picked up a live starfish, tossed it back into the ocean and said, *"I think it mattered to that one."*

Many emotionally, physically, sexually, and spiritually wounded people identify with this story. They too see themselves as being washed up from life's storms and left to die on some forgotten shore. They cannot find their way back to the life-giving ocean where they can thrive once again. Yet the actions of one person can make a difference for generations to come:

One hundred years from now,
It won't matter what car I drove,
What kind of house I lived in,
How much I had in my bank account,
Nor what my clothes looked like,
But, the world may be a little better
Because I was important in the life of a child.

Unknown

THE DESCENT

The Journey is Just Beginning

A common misperception about coming down from a mountain-top experience, literally or spiritually, is believing that the journey, let alone the transformative experience, is over. Admittedly, we may feel as though the task of ascending the mountain is behind us and now that we are at the base again, we can revel in a job well done, or at least admire the pictures we have taken. But just as I discovered when coming down from Bear Butte, my transformative journey was just beginning. Indeed there were many spiritual insights I needed to integrate. One question in particular was *"Where is this transformative experience going to take me?"*

Many people often romanticize spiritual encounters with God. Enthralled by listening to the sensational stories and cryptic experiences of others, some people use them as a template to measure their own spiritual experiences by. However, we must keep in mind that since each of us is unique, our spiritual experiences with God will also be unique to us. For example, thirteenth century Franciscan philosopher/theologian John Duns Scotus (1266-1308) was fond of using the term *haecceitas*, which denotes the discrete, God-imparted qualities, or characteristics, which make them unique persons. Uniqueness certainly includes being made in the image of God, but also involves a person's own distinct personality, gifts, talents, skills, and "this-ness". For example,

> LORD, *our Lord, how majestic is your name in all the earth! You have set your glory in the heavens.*

135

Through the praise of children and infants you have established a stronghold against your enemies, to silence the foe and the avenger. When I consider your heavens, the work of your fingers, the moon and the stars, which you have set in place, what is mankind that you are mindful of them, human beings that you care for them? You have made them a little lower than the angels and crowned them with glory and honor. You made them rulers over the works of your hands; you put everything under their feet: all flocks and herds, and the animals of the wild, the birds in the sky, and the fish in the sea, all that swim the paths of the seas. LORD, our Lord, how majestic is your name in all the earth!

Psalm 8

Indeed, we do not need to look around too long to understand that no two people are alike. Although we may have similar genetic features, our soul is unique to us just as fingerprints and snowflakes are to each other. And yet, part of reclaiming our authenticity involves both embracing our own uniqueness, as well as the responsibility to care for Creation. We are to take what has been transformed in us and be agents of transformation in the world in which we live. In *Man's Search For Meaning,* Frankl (1997) echoes this sentiment:

We must never forget that we may also find meaning in life when confronted with a hopeless situation, when facing a fate that cannot be changed. For what then matters is to bear witness to the uniquely

> *human potential at its best, which is to transform*
> *a personal tragedy into a triumph, to turn one's*
> *predicament into a human achievement.*

Therefore, let us not assume that by desiring psycho-spiritual transformation, namely drawing close to God, means that we will automatically have a life-changing encounter accompanied by miracles and whistles. We may and we may not. In fact, the opportunity to be transformed by God might occur when we least expect it. There's familiar story is recounted by Friar Thomas of Celano (1200-1265) regarding Francis of Assisi's encounter with a man with leprosy. Little did Francis know that when he transcended his personal limitations and assumptions, he went from seeing a miserable wretch of a leprous man, to embracing a person full of dignity and worth. Thus, he could no longer hold back the spiritual transformation that was unfolding in him:

> *When Francis was a young man, after he had*
> *decided that he did not wish to be a cloth merchant*
> *like his father, after his dream of knighthood had*
> *been crushed by a prolonged illness, and before he*
> *discerned his vocation in life, it is told that he was*
> *walking along a road on the outskirts of Assisi with*
> *his friend, Leo, when he thought he heard a bell.*
> *It was not the bright sound of a church bell, but*
> *rather a coarse, flat tone like a cowbell. Francis*
> *was frightened by this sound because it was*
> *unpleasant, yet familiar. The sound started to come*
> *closer and closer. His friend Leo realized what the*

sound meant. "Let's get out of here, Francis," Leo cried. But Francis, not knowing exactly why, stood his ground. Leo pleaded again, but Francis, now trembling, would not run. Suddenly, over the hill just ahead, there appeared a deformed figure with a clanging bell around his neck. Francis' heart pounded. His nostrils burned with a pungent smell of rotting flesh. The figure waved him off, but Francis did not move. "A leper," he thought to himself. "I have always been repulsed by the sight of lepers! How much I have feared their dreaded contagion!" "Have you not heard my bell?" asked the leper. "Do you know I am forced to wear this bell to warn you that a leper is approaching?" Francis remained motionless, tasting his fear as he swallowed. Then suddenly, filled with a strength which came he knew not from where, Francis ran toward the leper, now much more frightened than he. Francis embraced the leper, kissed him on his festering cheek, and wept aloud, "Brother leper, forgive me for neglecting you." Then, for a moment, he seemed to wear a crown of thorns and to bleed from his wounds in his hands, his feet and his sides. He looked at Francis with love. And then, just as suddenly, the leper vanished from sight, leaving Francis weeping on the silent road. Francis had found his calling.

The First Life of St. Francis, pp. 231-35.

When considering transformation and transcendence I used to wonder which came first (This is kind of a chicken-egg question)? Do we experience transformation first then transcend our surroundings, limitations and personal boundaries, or like Francis is it when we transcend these limitations that we are transformed? Regardless of whether we have experienced spiritual transformation before transcending our boundaries (self-imposed or otherwise), or we have experienced transcendence prior to spiritual transformation, the two are intertwined and connected. This spiritual relationship always reminds me of the Tango, which has been described as an energetic, passionate, and playful dance filled with artistic expression. In both modern and traditional Tango styles, once dancers have mastered the moves involved, they can spend endless hours lost in this vibrant dance. In fact, the beauty of watching the Tango is the fluidity of the dance; two dancers magically become one on the dance floor. Therefore, simply put, you cannot have transformation without transcendence and vice versa. It is a both/and phenomena initiated by God that requires an active dance partner. While it is true that the on-going transformation comes in God's timing we must also avail ourselves in what John Wesley referred to as the "means of grace." In the United Methodist tradition, this phrase means that once we have experienced God's Spirit in our lives, we therefore, live in the light of this Spirit as we devote ourselves to prayer, fellowship, outreach, meditative reflection, Scripture study, spiritual ceremonies, participation in the sacraments, worship, and other acts of devotion. When we open ourselves up, sometimes simply by just showing up to hear God more clearly in our lives, God extends grace for us to be transformed.

As we transform, we transcend previous limitations, which prepares us for further transformation, transcendence, and so on.

In Buddhism there is a famous painting that tells a story about how an ox-herder follows the path toward enlightenment or spiritual awareness. To the western mind, it might be difficult at first to see ourselves in the image of the herder who is seeking spiritual awareness which is represented by the ox. However, once we understand the concept, we will see that attaining enlightenment or spiritual awareness is not a passive event. For example:

> The first of the pictures depicts the man setting out in search of an ox. He then proceeds to follow the ox by following the footprints in the snow. He then discovers the ox and gets ready to catch it. After this the man is riding the ox while playing a trumpet. This picture most likely is depicting that the man has successfully tamed the bull, and has made peace with it. The following picture shows the man alone, sitting down, left behind once the ox had transcended. The next picture frame shows nothing, suggesting that both the ox and man had transcended. The ninth of the ten pictures shows a tree, most likely depicting paradise that the man has achieved through his conquering of the ox. The last of the pictures shows him teaching his methods to others, showing to them how they too can accomplish what he had.

As previously stated, this picture story is a symbol for a person's path to enlightenment in which the ox is a metaphor for humanity's struggle finding their inner self. The taming of the ox in the story is a depiction of the man coming to terms with his authentic self, which allows him to advance in the path to enlightenment or spiritual awareness. Once he has fulfilled this objective in life, he is at peace and transcends into full spiritual awareness. As a result, his obligation now is to teach his ways to others, aiding them in their path to enlightenment or spiritual awareness (Wada, 2002). Understanding this process is vital to embracing our desire to live authentically. We may not imagine ourselves as herders chasing an ox, but I believe we do appreciate the need to pursue the desires for genuineness in life. Moreover, once we are engaged in the search for authenticity and reclaim it for ourselves, we are then obligated to aid others in the quest as well.

In training pastoral counseling students I often stress to them a similar analogy: If they (including faculty) are faithful to the process of integrating their spiritual growth with their clinical knowledge and skills; transformation and transcendence is inevitable. For example, I often look forward to our end of the year graduation celebration our Pastoral Counseling/Spiritual Direction programs host. That evening is a wonderful time of celebration, reminiscing and congratulating those who have reached the graduation mile-stone in their lives. Yet, what makes this evening so special is that there is a time when graduating students share the experiences over the past four years. No matter how unique their stories are, there is a common thread that emerges, namely the fact that they are not the same persons that they were prior to beginning the program; something has changed in them. Indeed, as they were faithful to the process of the personal and professional integration of their studies, spirituality, personal counseling and clinical experience, they noticed their own spiritual transformation. Although they may not be able to point to an exact time when their transformation occurred in the program, they have discovered how their authentic presence in mental health has helped them transcend their growing edges as counselors in training. This transformation is often acknowledged with great humility and reverence by faculty and staff as well, as we acknowledge their readiness to pursue national certification, state licensure, and/ or additional training/supervision.

As previously mentioned, psycho-spiritual transformation is initiated in us through God's Spirit, but it does not necessarily depend all on God. We also have a responsibility in continuing the process in all areas of our lives. The following questions help cultivate spiritual awareness throughout this process:

- *Are we paying attention the lessons revealed to us about ourselves; our assumptions, choices and behaviors?*
- *Which lessons are familiar to us and which ones are new?*
- *Are we asking honest questions about our inauthentic ways without making excuses or shifting blame to another?*
- *Are we able to distinguish clearly what we need to own for ourselves, verses what others are responsible for?*
- *What is keeping us from totally surrendering to God?*

- *What are we afraid of letting go of in order to take hold of something better?*
- *What parts of us needs to be healed?*
- *Are there parts of ourselves we have yet to integrate?*
- *What relationships do we need to heal?*
- *Are there people in our lives (living or deceased) whom we need to say "forgive me, I forgive you, thank you and/or I love you?"*(Byock, 2004)

Ironically, taking responsibility for sustaining our psycho-spiritual health also runs parallel to us taking care of our physical health. For example, people who have had bypass surgery to remove blockages in the arteries of the heart are now responsible for sustaining their health through a change in diet, exercise, proper medication regimen, even lowering cholesterol and eliminating stress. Unfortunately, if these behaviors and perhaps more importantly unsafe attitudes towards their health do not change, they will likely continue building up blockages again. This analogy of building up blockages in the heart is also true in our spiritual and emotional lives. Once we have had an encounter with God and our spiritual eyes have been opened, we must commit to changes in our attitudes and behaviors in order to sustain our healing transformation. It is not enough for us to rely on a one-time transformative encounter with God and expect that experience to carry us through the rest of our lives in terms of our psycho-spiritual growth. In fact, I believe just the opposite is true. For instance, I have often wondered how differently people live their lives after their prayers have been answered following a revival or healing service:

- Do they return home the same person that they were before being healed?
- Do they notice any kind of emotional changes occurring in them?
- For some being healed might involve surrendering physical disability claims or handicapped parking stickers?
- Do they now look forward to seeking employment that was perhaps denied to them because of their disability?
- Do they now treat people differently (being more forgiving, understanding, and patient), and do they find that others treat them differently?
- Along with their physical illness, are people also healed from any co-dependent or self-defeating attitudes?
- When does the mind, with all of its assumptions, catch up with the transformation that has occurred physically, emotionally, and/or spiritually?

A New Name, Identity and Walk

I am a firm believer that in order to sustain changes in our lives this involves the courage to let go of the former familiar and allow the transformation of ourselves to unfold. I agree with authors Roberts and Levy (2008) who say that people are more likely to transform and continue their transformation when they are committed to, and involved with, their own healing process.

In other words, we need to take an active integrative approach to *unlearning* negative attitudes, old habits, and inauthenticity, while at the same time *relearning* or *reclaiming our authenticity* in life-giving ways that sustain our physical, emotional and spiritual healing. In the Book of Genesis (chapters 25-33), Jacob is such an example of this unlearning/learning psycho-spiritual transformation and transcendence. For example, prior to his life-changing encounter with God, Jacob's life was the epitome of the *"I'll do it myself"* mentality. As the son of Isaac and the grandson of Abraham, Jacob was aware of God's covenantal promises of land and descendants made to Abraham's line:

> *Jacob left Beersheba and set out for Harran. When he reached a certain place, he stopped for the night because the sun had set. Taking one of the stones there, he put it under his head and lay down to sleep. He had a dream in which he saw a stairway resting on the earth, with its top reaching to heaven, and the angels of God were ascending and descending on it. There above it stood the LORD, and he said: "I am the LORD, the God of your father Abraham and the God of Isaac. I will give you and your descendants the land on which you are lying. Your descendants will be like the dust of the earth, and you will spread out to the west and to the east, to the north and to the south. All peoples on earth will be blessed through you and your offspring. I am with you and will watch over you wherever you go, and I will bring you back to this land. I will not leave you until*

I have done what I have promised you." When Jacob
awoke from his sleep, he thought, "Surely the LORD
is in this place, and I was not aware of it." He was
afraid and said, "How awesome is this place! This
is none other than the house of God; this is the gate
of heaven." Early the next morning Jacob took the
stone he had placed under his head and set it up as
a pillar and poured oil on top of it. He called that
place Bethel though the city used to be called Luz.

Genesis 28:10-18

Just as the expression goes that *the apple doesn't fall from the tree*, Jacob tried to secure God's covenant through his accomplishments (similar to Abraham and Isaac); often the result of being a shrewd businessman. Granted, Jacob prospered in all that he did, but in terms of walking authentically before God and others, he needed to learn what living authentically demanded of him before claiming his place in God's covenant. Furthermore, it was time for Jacob to fully realize *the more than what he knew* in himself, as well as the responsibilities. This undertaking was not without its struggle:

That night Jacob got up and took his two wives, his two
female servants and his eleven sons and crossed the
ford of the Jabbok. After he had sent them across the
stream, he sent over all his possessions. So Jacob was
left alone, and a man wrestled with him till daybreak.
When the man saw that he could not overpower him,
he touched the socket of Jacob's hip so that his hip
was wrenched as he wrestled with the man.

*Then the man said, "Let me go, for it is daybreak."
But Jacob replied, "I will not let you go unless
you bless me." The man asked him, "What is your
name?" "Jacob," he answered. Then the man said,
"Your name will no longer be Jacob, but Israel,
because you have struggled with God and with
humans and have overcome."*

*Jacob said, "Please tell me your name." But he
replied, "Why do you ask my name?" Then he
blessed him there. So Jacob called the place Peniel,
saying, "It is because I saw God face to face, and
yet my life was spared." The sun rose above him
as he passed Peniel, and he was limping because
of his hip. Therefore to this day the Israelites do
not eat the tendon attached to the socket of the hip,
because the socket of Jacob's hip was touched near
the tendon.*

Genesis 32:22-32

That night, Jacob underwent a powerful transformation
that integrated his new name, a new identity and a new walk.
He went from being concerned only about himself (*Jacob=one
who supersedes*) to claiming something greater than him for the
sake of future generations (*Israel=one who struggles/governs
with God*). Moreover, Jacob's new name now indicates the
nature of his new relationship with God. His identity is now
grounded in the covenantal lineage of those who came before
him (Abraham and Isaac), as well as future generations that
would claim his name, identity and walk before God.

Everyone who has experienced the touch of God in a radical, life-transforming manner always wants to experience more of God. Whatever the spiritual experience was, the tiniest spark of God's Spirit ignites an unquenchable flame in us to desire more and more of the Spirit. The task then is for us to fan the flames into a change in behaviors, mindset and devotion to God, which, as a result of living more authentically, is to express humility in our relationships with ourselves, others, and God. We are certainly more than what we realize, and yet when we are ready to walk authentically, similar to Jacob, we will know who we are and whose we are.

Still, many people wonder why psycho-spiritual transformation can be painful at times. The answer is simple but the implications are profound. Perhaps the reason why we experience difficulty during our psycho-spiritual transformation is we do not often allow ourselves enough time to discern, let alone integrate what has happened to us. For the most part, integration is a life-long process of living out our authenticity in this world. However, there are some practical things we can do following divine encounters. For example, after spending hours in prayer, spiritual ceremonies, contemplating and experiencing the touch of God, we may feel as though we are floating somewhere in the universe. Before our spiritual feet are back on the ground, we may want to rush right back into a daily routine. Little do we realize that we may be doing more harm than good? Spiritual work especially on this level has the potential to be physically and emotionally exhausting. As a result, we need to allow ourselves time to rest, reflect and recharge. Some people are physically exhausted and need to sleep. Other people need time to process what has shifted in them. Some people share a simple meal in order to further "digest" the wisdom and insights people may have encountered. Regardless of the experience, self-care is a must!

Ironically, some people report experiencing an emotional release or let down following their psycho-spiritual mountaintop experience. They may sob, become depressed and even nauseated. I often refer to this phenomenon as the Elijah Syndrome, which is taken from the prophet Elijah's own experience as recorded in book of 1 Kings. According to the story, Elijah had a powerful mountain top experience with the Spirit of God when he confronted the prophets of Baal. For lack of a better description, this encounter was more like a showdown between two fighters (1 Kings 18:16ff). Once the divine encounter was over, the triumphant Elijah descended into an emotional depression that left him doubting whether or not God was ever with him? For example,

> *Now Ahab told Jezebel everything Elijah had done and how he had killed all the prophets with the sword. So Jezebel sent a messenger to Elijah to say, "May the gods deal with me, be it ever so severely, if by this time tomorrow I do not make your life like that of one of them." Elijah was afraid and ran for his life. When he came to Beersheba in Judah, he left his servant there, while he himself went a day's journey into the wilderness. He came to a broom bush, sat down under it and prayed that he might*

die. "I have had enough, LORD," he said. "Take my life; I am no better than my ancestors." Then he lay down under the bush and fell asleep.

All at once an angel touched him and said, "Get up and eat." He looked around, and there by his head was some bread baked over hot coals, and a jar of water. He ate and drank and then lay down again. The angel of the LORD came back a second time and touched him and said, "Get up and eat, for the journey is too much for you." So he got up and ate and drank. Strengthened by that food, he traveled forty days and forty nights until he reached Horeb, the mountain of God. There he went into a cave and spent the night.

And the word of the LORD came to him: "What are you doing here, Elijah?" He replied, "I have been very zealous for the LORD God Almighty. The Israelites have rejected your covenant, torn down your altars, and put your prophets to death with the sword. I am the only one left, and now they are trying to kill me too." The LORD said, "Go out and stand on the mountain in the presence of the LORD, for the LORD is about to pass by." Then a great and powerful wind tore the mountains apart and shattered the rocks before the LORD, but the LORD was not in the wind. After the wind there was an earthquake, but the LORD was not in the earthquake. After the earthquake came a fire, but the LORD was not in the fire. And after the fire came a gentle

whisper. When Elijah heard it, he pulled his cloak
over his face and went out and stood at the mouth of
the cave. Then a voice said to him, "What are you
doing here, Elijah?"

He replied, "I have been very zealous for the LORD
God Almighty. The Israelites have rejected your
covenant, torn down your altars, and put your
prophets to death with the sword. I am the only one
left, and now they are trying to kill me too." The
LORD said to him, "Go back the way you came, and
go to the Desert of Damascus. When you get there,
anoint Hazael king over Aram. Also, anoint Jehu
son of Nimshi king over Israel, and anoint Elisha
son of Shaphat from Abel Meholah to succeed you
as prophet. Jehu will put to death any who escape
the sword of Hazael, and Elisha will put to death
any who escape the sword of Jehu. Yet I reserve
seven thousand in Israel—all whose knees have not
bowed down to Baal and whose mouths have not
kissed him."

Living In Awareness

Down through the ages it was a common belief that once people
had experienced any sort of psycho-spiritual transformation
this meant that they were immediately drawn into seclusion,
away from their communities. Many people fled to monasteries,
convents or other isolated parts of the world, in order to
further cultivate their spiritual awareness. Today, this practice

can no longer be assumed. In fact, while psycho-spiritually transformative encounters with God do indeed pull us away from the perceptions of a linear thinking worldview, we discover that our transcendence leads us back into our communities to authentically serve others. For example, Bodo (2007) states:

> *This inner absorption in God does not keep the saint inside, rapt in God and unaware of others. It may for a while during a time of ecstasy or inner vision, but inevitably absorption in God leads to a greater perception of outward things that makes of the saint and mystic one who serves and loves others to a heroic degree. Charity is what makes saints and mystics, not the inner visions, marvels and miracles. 'Faith, hope and love abide', St. Paul says, 'and the greatest of these is love'*
>
> (1 Corinthians 13:13).

Becoming aware of God's presence in our lives perhaps through a life-changing psycho-spiritual transformation, is actually for some people their first step toward self-awareness. In fact, I have noticed that the first place a psycho-spiritual transformation becomes evident to us is in our prayer life and daily devotion to God.

> *O Great Spirit, whose breath gives life to the world, and whose voice is heard in the soft breeze: We need your strength and wisdom. Cause us to walk in beauty. Give us eyes ever to behold the red and purple sunset. Make us wise so that we*

may understand what you have taught us. Help us learn the lessons you have hidden in every leaf and rock. Make us always ready to come to you with clean hands and steady eyes, so when life fades, like the fading sunset, our spirits come to your without shame.

A Traditional Native American Prayer,
United Methodist Hymnal, #329

Becoming fully aware of God's presence in our lives is a relentless commitment to listening for God each day in the ordinary (Wicks, 1995). In his book entitled, *Care of the Soul,* contemporary psychotherapist Thomas Moore (1994) echoes Wicks by saying that *by learning to discover and value our ordinariness, we nurture a friendliness toward ourselves and the world that is the essence of a healthy soul.* In her book, *The Humility of God: A Franciscan Perspective,* Ilea Delio (2009) highlights how service to others in love is modeled through the irony of the Cross. She states, *God has demonstrated that through the outward appearance of weakness and powerlessness of the Cross, it is the very power of love to heal and transform death into life. In this image, humanity understands the posture of God; one who has transcended his world and bends down to share our suffering, so that we may be caught up in God's embrace.* This example of transcendent humility on behalf of God provides us a clear implication for us to embrace our own humility as a motivation to reach out to others in service. Trappist monk Thomas Merton (1915-1968) affirms the need for humility in service:

It is almost impossible to overestimate the value of true humility and its power in the spiritual life. For the beginning of humility is the beginning of blessedness and the consummation of humility is the perfection of all joy. Humility contains in itself the answer to all the great problems of the life of the soul. It is the only key to faith, with which the spiritual life begins: for faith and humility are inseparable. In perfect humility all selfishness disappears and your soul no longer lives for itself or in itself for God: and it is lost and submerged in Him and transformed into Him."

– "New Seeds of Contemplation"(2007)

Perhaps one of the most important aspects in cultivating humility is that it protects people from perceiving themselves as the privileged ones who have all the answers. Instead, humility compels us to ask poignant questions from ourselves:

- While I serve others, how can I help them maintain their dignity?
- What are the specific ways I can serve others without making them feel inferior?
- Are there specific issues within society itself whereby my service may be more of a burden than a benefit? (McAlpin, 2009).
- How am I hindering another person's spiritual growth by enabling them to remain dependent on a broken economic, political or religious system?

- How does my service empower others to then go back and help others?
- How does my service encourage others to live more authentically?
- How does receiving another's service, encourages me to live more authentically?

Indeed, it takes tremendous courage to ask these and other questions related to our motivation of giving and receiving. Nonetheless, spiritual reflection affords us the opportunity and the grace for self-discovery in the midst of human need. Through the stillness of contemplation and reflection on our experiences we become aware of the importance of being faithful to the integrative process, and how we are being transformed into more authentic, humble persons of faith. Spiritual reflection takes tremendous courage, because at times we must face both the mystery of self-discovery and the misery of human suffering. Through the stillness of contemplation and reflection we become aware of the voices within reminding us of our own weaknesses, wounds, scars, desires, strengths, fears, frailty, resiliency, goals, limitations, motivations and growing edges. Yet this insight is not by accident because the goal of spiritual reflection is transformation into a more authentic person and thus, compels us ultimately towards transcending ourselves in order to have a more effective service to others in the spirit of humility.

Many people who have been emotionally and physically wounded in relationships are often hypersensitive when they perceive others acting inauthentic towards them in the present.

Feelings of distrust, suspicion and humiliation often leave them very protective of the wounds of their broken promises, dreams, and lives. In fact, depending on the depth of people's wounds (and scars), some do not even bother to invest what little energy they have if they believe their friendship and trust will not be valued, let alone reciprocated. People simply will not risk being made to feel vulnerable again. For example, in the book *Same Kind of Different As Me*, authors Ron Hall and Denver Moore (2006) recount a story about vulnerability and trust at the beginning of their friendship. One of them made the offer of friendship. The other's mind was on going fishing:

> *If you is fishin for a friend you just gon' catch and release, then I ain't got no desire to be your friend. . .but if you is lookin for a real friend, then I'll be one. Forever."*

People have had enough of being used and abused in their lives to know when someone is acting with ulterior motives. But when genuineness is displayed, relationships take on a powerful bond that weathers the most sensitive feelings of vulnerability. Recognizing and valuing what people have to offer one another only strengthens this bond.

The Hollow Bone: Listening With the Heart

In the Oglala Lakota tradition, Frank Fools Crow (1890 – 1989) taught that in order to become holy, i.e., one through whom the Great Spirit could work in and through to heal others, a person must become like a *hollow bone*. Fools Crow believed that people are not to seek transformation for their own power and honor, but instead to be a pipeline that connects God (*Wakan Tanka*) and the people. This process of becoming a hollow bone began when people asked *Wakan Tanka* to rid themselves of anything that would impede them in any way, such as doubt, questions, selfishness or reluctance. As a result, psycho-spiritually transformed people would then need to see themselves as unobstructed conduits through whom God could work to bless others.

The hollow bone is a powerful symbol for emptying ourselves of everything that hinders and impedes the life of the God's Spirit. As we were taught in biology class, bones provide our bodies not only with our physical frame, but also within themselves, contain marrow (flexible tissue) that is responsible for producing blood and supporting the immune system. However, in understanding the concept of becoming a hollow bone, we must first acknowledge our need to, *metaphorically speaking*, die to ourselves. Ironically, a hollow bone is both dead, in that it does not contain any blood or marrow, and at the same time, is alive because it is the Spirit of God flowing freely in and through us for the benefit of others. This act is not a one-time event, but rather an-going process of examining and letting go of ourselves in order to take hold of something better for the sake of humanity (Coyhis, 2007).

God is speaking all the time. What keep us from hearing His voice? Through contemplation we not only we need to stop our mind's chatter, but also to open our hearts regarding how we see and listen for God. Where do we see God in all things? In the beauty of a sunrise and the suns glow at a sunset? Do we focus on hearing God's voice in their cries and laughter of others? How do we feel God in the wind and rain? Do we hear God in the sound of owls, eagles and hawks? Similarly, should we not also look for God in the tears of a child, or listen for the voice of God in every heartbreak, or find the voice of God giving us a voice to express our losses?

> *One day when we came back from work, we saw three gallows rearing up in the assembly place, three black crows. Roll call. SS all around us, machine guns trained: the traditional ceremony. Three victims in chains and one of them, the little servant, the sad-eyed angel. The SS seemed more preoccupied, more disturbed than usual. To hang a young boy in front of thousands of spectators was no light matter. The head of the camp read the verdict. All eyes were on the child. He was lividly pale, almost calm, biting his lips. The gallows threw its shadow over him. This time the Lagerkapo refused to act as executioner. Three SS replaced him.*

> *The three victims mounted together onto the chairs. The three necks were placed at the same moment within the nooses. "Long live liberty!" cried the two adults. But the child was silent. "Where is God? Where is He?" someone behind me asked. At a sign from the head of the camp, the three chairs tipped over. Total silence throughout the camp. On the*

horizon, the sun was setting. "Bare your heads!"
yelled the head of the camp. His voice was raucous.
We were weeping. "Cover your heads!" Then the
march past began. The two adults were no longer
alive. Their tongues hung swollen, blue-tinged. But
the third rope was still moving; being so light, the
child was still alive... For more than half an hour
he stayed there, struggling between life and death,
dying in slow agony under our eyes. And we had to
look him full in the face. He was still alive when I
passed in front of him. His tongue was red, his eyes
were not yet glazed. Behind me, I heard the same
man asking: "Where is God now?" And I heard a
voice within me answer him: "Where is He? Here
He is—He is hanging here on this gallows..."

Night, Elie Weisel (2006)

The more attuned we are with the presence of God, the more we experience the *empathetic resonance,* (Sardello, 2009) i.e., the resonance of our soul coming into the resonance with the Soul of God. What we discover in being more fully connected to the Soul of God then, is that we are connected to things that bring us great joy, as well as being connected to things that are disturbing and cause us great suffering. Still, we embrace all to be an extension of God's presence, grace and healing for people who are looking and listening for God's presence, grace and healing. In other words, we embrace *all things* in order to create a space for transformation to occur in *all persons.*

As transformed people we cannot pick and choose when, where, why, and how God will use us. Instead, since we expect that God is more than able to understand and embrace all aspects of our lives, then should we not be willing to be the same for ourselves and others? If we want to be used by God as healers it should not come as a surprise that we will placed in circumstances where there is pain, sorrow and suffering. If we want God to grant us ancient wisdom it should come as no surprise that we will be placed in situations where people are impulsive and lack insight. If we want God to use us as peacemakers it should be no surprise that we will be placed in times of war, chaos and death. In fact, to work for peace we may have to expose ourselves to non-peaceful situations. The same is true in that if we work to be more and more authentic, then we find ourselves at times being exposed to inauthentic people and situations. The question for us then, is when we listen for God, what do we hear?

The Legend of the American Indian Courting Flute, Wapp, 1984.

> *Suddenly there was an entirely new sound, the kind neither he nor any other man had ever experienced before. It was very mournful, sad, and ghostlike. In a way it made the hunter afraid, so he drew his robe tightly about him and reached for his bow, to make sure that it was properly strung. On the other hand, this new sound was like a song, beautiful beyond imagination, full of love, hope, yearning. And then,*

*before he knew it, and with the night more than half
gone, he was suddenly asleep. He dreamed that a
bird called wagnuka, the redheaded woodpecker,
appeared to him, singing the strangely beautiful
new song, saying, "Follow me and I will teach you."*

*When he awoke he found a cedar tree. He broke
off a branch, and working many hours hollowed
it out delicately with a bow-string drill. Just as he
had seen wagnuka do it in his vision. He whittled
the branch into a shape of a bird with a long neck
and an open beak. He painted the top of the bird's
head red with washasha, the sacred vermilion color.
He prayed. He smoked the branch with incense
of burning sage and sweet grass. He fingered the
holes as he had watched it done in his dream, all
the while blowing softly into the end of his flute.
Because this is what he had made - the first flute,
the very first siyotanka. And all at once there was
the song, ghostlike and beautiful beyond words, and
all the people were astounded and joyful. And that
is how siyotanka the flute came to be -- thanks to
the cedar, the woodpecker, the wind and one young
hunter who shot no elk but who knew how to listen.*

The American Indian courting flute:
Revitalization and change, Contemporary
American Indian Issues Series, Number
5, *Sharing a Heritage: American
Indian Arts, edited by Charlotte Heth
and Michael Swarm*, 49–60.

Throughout history, sages and mystics have all communicated that the best way to listen to God in the ordinariness of our lives is though contemplative prayer. For many people (myself included), this is easier said than done. When I was in graduate school I was having lunch with several fellow pastors. After a few bites into my sandwich the topic of conversation turned to prayer. In between bites of food and sips of coffee, we shared our unique way of talking to God. Some preferred early morning devotions, others preferred nighttime. Me, I bragged about how much I talked to God all day long. I could talk to God in the morning, afternoon, and evening. As I was going on and on, I noticed a colleague of mine from Kenya sitting across from me with folded arms and a look of disappointment on his face. When I finished he looked straight at me and accused me of knowing nothing about prayer. I was shocked (and a little offended). With all the wounded pride I could muster, I replied that I most certainly knew about prayer, and began to quote chapter and verse about the benefit of praying without ceasing (1 Thessalonians 5:17). In mid-sentence my friend held up his hand to stop me and declared that what I was saying was actually the problem . . . I did all the talking. I never stopped and listened to what God might want to say to me. Good point. He was right. Welcome to my first lesson in contemplative prayer. Admittedly, I knew nothing about this contemplative style of praying. In my mind I believed prayer was communicating to God. Furthermore, I believed that I was very good at petitionary prayer, i.e, prayer that involves some sort of request such as to give thanks, sometimes to praise, sometimes to apologize and seek forgiveness, and sometimes to ask for things for myself. Little did I understand over this lunchtime conversation that it was actually God who wanted to communicate with me? From that point on I felt myself slowly falling in love with contemplative prayer; a quieting of my mind and opening myself up to allow my spirit to communicate with the Holy Spirit. To my delight, I not only started to recognize more of God's presence in my life, but also I began to understand how my own inner chatter wooed me away from hearing what I needed to hear from God.

Listening to another speak is not as easy as it sounds. In fact, listening while being fully present to the person (and God), is actually becoming a lost art in society. In everyday conversations many people simply wait to talk without really listening to what is being said. They may very politely wait for their turn to speak, but do not hear with their hearts, let alone consider the impact of the other person's words. This certainly includes our conversations with God. However, when prayer is infused with contemplation, we enter into a receptive, deep method of silent prayer in which we experience God's presence within us and all around us (Keating, 2009). Still, this type of prayer is never meant to replace other kinds of prayer, such as intercessory prayer, but rather, contemplation adds depth of meaning to all prayer, and is essential when we feel disconnected, afraid, or simply out of control. Moreover, contemplation helps us reclaim our authentic selves as the silence awakens the deepest desires of our soul.

Before I fully understood the value of contemplation, I viewed silence as not only the absence of noise, but also the absence of God. To be quite honest, I knew that silence was there, but I did not know how to enter it, or how to listen for God in the silence. My mind and ego could not comprehend how God communicates when I hear nothing. In fact, in some ways I was like David in Psalm 22:1-3, *My God, my God, why have you forsaken me? Why are you so far from saving me, so far from my cries of anguish? My God, I cry out by day, but you do not answer, by night, but I find no rest.* Although, most people are uncomfortable with silence or convince themselves that God is uninterested in their circumstances, silence is actually where we connect with the living presence of God. For example, we do not enter into the silence just for the sake of ridding ourselves of whatever sounds of the day we want to escape. Many people would see this as a welcomed relief. On the contrary, we purposefully enter into the silence with God in order to experience this *empathetic resonance* more clearly.

To further grasp this truth, contemplate the silence of water. If you have ever noticed, water is the epitome of silence. Water only makes sound when it is moving against another surface; being poured into a glass, as we swallow it, running over rocks or crashing against the shore when the wind creates its waves. And yet when it is still, the inaudible silence of water communicates how it is filled with life that gives life to all who depend on it. For example, the next time we drink water, meditate on the sound that it makes. Contemplate how the molecular structure of water (H_2O) gives life to our human breath (O_2 and CO_2).

Now consider how God has breathed life in us (Genesis 2:7) and where we feel the *breath, matter and movement* of God in our life. To take this understanding one step further, as we swallow water let us ask God how the essence of water helps us discover our inner voice so that we can be a voice for those who have no water, let alone who are unable to speak.

My colleague and friend, Fr. Sanjai Devis, also uses the image of water to tell a story of how both the *Sea of Galilee* and the *Dead Sea* can awaken us to a more practical application of authentic service toward others:

> *During my seminary training, I remember how fascinated I was when we were being taught all about the Dead Sea. As you probably might recall, the Dead Sea is really a Lake, not a sea (and as my teacher pointed out, if you understood that, it would guarantee four marks in the term paper!) It's so high in salt content that the human body can float easily. You can almost lie down and read a book! The salt in the Dead Sea is as high as 35% - almost 10 times the normal ocean water. And all that saltiness has meant that there is no life at all in the Dead Sea. No fish. No vegetation. No sea animals. Nothing lives in the Dead Sea. And hence the name: Dead Sea.*
>
> *I also learned about the Sea of Galilee. So when I heard about the Sea of Galilee and the Dead Sea and the tale of the two seas - I was intrigued. The Sea of Galilee is just north of the Dead Sea. Both the Sea of Galilee and the Dead Sea receive their*

water from river Jordan. And yet, they are very, very different. Unlike the Dead Sea, the Sea of Galilee is pretty, resplendent with rich, colorful marine life. There are lots of plants, trees, shrubs, and fish too. In fact, the Sea of Galilee is home to over twenty different types of fish.

Same region, same source of water, and yet while one sea is full of life, the other is dead. The River Jordan flows into the Sea of Galilee and then flows out. There is an inlet and an outlet. The water passes through the Sea of Galilee - in and then out - and that keeps the Sea healthy and vibrant, teeming with marine life. But the Dead Sea is far below the sea level, and it has no outlet. The water flows in from the river Jordan, but does not flow out. Tons of water evaporates from the Dead Sea every day, leaving it salty, full of minerals. And unfit for any marine life. No life at all. These two seas are symbols of human life.

Sometimes we might encounter people in our lives who are like the Dead Sea. Those who receive lot of blessings from God and others, but live a selfish life. People who use their wealth, health, knowledge, talents given by God for one's own self, those who do not share. They become dead like the Dead Sea; there is no life within them, because there is no outlet. If we do not share it, it will become stale.

We also encounter people who are like the Sea of Galilee, those who receive love and give out love.

God is the source of love. When we open our hearts to him, our lives to him, we receive that love; we are filled with that love. Once we are filled with that love, we let it flow into other people. So every time it is fresh. We are filled and we give it away and again we are filled. Therefore, if we let God's love flow into us and we let it flow into other people, our lives will be like the Sea of Galilee. Husbands, wives, parents, children, priests, religious, those in helping professions and ministries are great examples of Sea of Galilee.

As people in ministry, people in helping professions - called to do God's work through our counseling professions, religious life, priesthood, apostolate, we could probably identify ourselves more with the Sea of Galilee than with the Dead Sea. We love to give and to share ourselves with God and his people. We are always giving. Our lives are like the Sea of Galilee. We become the river banks that become places of consolation and grace for other people - the people we are in touch with, we relate with, we care for, we make friends with. And they experience God's love, consolation & healing in and through us. Probably what we deal with in our life is that we find difficult to balance the act of receiving and giving.

What happens if Sea of Galilee gives out more water than the amount of water it receives? It will go dry. Probably in our life, ministry and profession, this could happen to us. We might stretch ourselves too thin that we go dry. We need to be constantly nurtured to go on giving. I experience this many times in my work at the hospital and in the parish. It speaks of the need for self-care that we constantly read and speak about. Therefore, as often as we give, we will also need to refill it. It is to be recharged so that we can give more, or continue giving. In John's gospel 15:16, Jesus reminds us, "I have chosen you to bear fruits, fruit that will last." For our fruits to last, we need constant recharging. Otherwise we will be drained out.

Reclaiming Our Connectedness

One of the most profound teachings among the value of living an authentic life in humility is the understanding that all life is connected. From the air we breathe and water we drink, to the food we ingest and energy we consume, everything and everyone is linked to one another in a delicate harmony. And yet, connectedness is a measure of our feelings of belonging and responsibility we have to a larger human reality that cuts across generations and groups (Piedmont, 1999).

Most of the time, being interconnected is difficult for us to grasp because so many things in our lives vie for our individual attention. For example, in Western society as individualism is often valued, we may forget the important of interpersonal relationships. In fact, we often do not realize that our words, actions, and our very thoughts carry with them the ability to be both life giving and life-destroying. We so often do not see how we are connected but we are, even to all of Creation. Our intentions are felt throughout the world. So often teachings are now focused on negative behaviors impacting others around the world; a sociological-traumatic-globalization as it is. Furthermore, let us consider how many of our attitudes and behaviors might change if we embrace the idea that what we do today affects people seven generations from us. *Wellbriety Movement* founder Don Coyhis states:

> *What we do today will affect the children seven generations form now. How we treat the Mother Earth will affect the children yet to be born. If we poison the water today, our children's children will be affected by the decision we made. Our children are the gateway to the future. Let us conscientiously think about the children and the seven generations to come.*

To add another dimension to this understanding, let us consider the impact our lives would have today if we went back seven generations and expressed gratitude for the gifts we enjoy today. What sacrifices did our ancestors make? Did they realize the likelihood their decisions would have on us seven generations later?

In our present generation, I believe that we do not fully realize the potential of transforming lives we have been given. If we understand that our negative thoughts, words and actions have consequences, then how much more will our positive thoughts, words and actions be the medicine that gives life? If we really want to see change in the world, then psycho-spiritual transformation begins in us by transcending our perceived limitations. Author of the *Tao Te Ching* and sixth century Chinese philosopher Lao Tzu, echoes this notion:

> *If you want to awaken all of humanity then awaken all of yourself. If you want to eliminate the "suffering in the world, then eliminate all that is dark and negative in yourself. Truly, the greatest gift you have to give is that of your own self-transformation.*

When we reclaim our authentic selves, we also reclaim our connectedness to all living things. All of Creation is attuned to the heartbeat of God. It does not matter what generation we were born into, the fact is that we have been preceded in death by millions and will most likely be followed by countless future generations. As a result, we are mere stewards of what the Creator has entrusted to us. Living authentically requires us to understand that we are not our own; our thoughts and actions do have a direct influence on all living beings. Humility teaches us that when we do not honor our natural and/or spiritual resources as gifts from God, we tend to believe we have a right to dispose of them (and perhaps people) as we see fit. Throughout history such arrogance has slaughtered millions, left lands barren, and perpetuated generations plagued by emotional trauma. Authenticity on the other hand, produces tangible humility that is lived out in healing and wholeness, as well as plants seeds of peaceable redemption in past, present, and future generations.

Healing Generational Trauma

These days there is much public interest in searching family trees for links to our ancestors. Although, discovering the origins of our surnames and how our ancestors lived can be an exciting hobby, we may overlook what emotional or spiritual trauma has also been passed down through these generations that plague some people today. For example:

- Who struggled with addictions, relationships, their faith and/or employment?
- Is there any emotional and psychological evidence that some adults suffered from being a child of an alcoholic? Are there any symptoms of depression, anxiety or post-traumatic stress in the family?
- Was there any physical, psychological, or spiritual trauma? If so, who were the abusers and who were the victims/survivors?
- Were there any national, state or community tragedies that may have contributed to a family member's secondary trauma?
- Were there untimely deaths or suicides? How were they handled in the family?
- What generational secrets did families hold onto as their identity or shame?

Although these questions identify a few characteristics that contemporary families deal with, such phenomenon has been shown to be communicated through the generations as families tell and retell their stories through their behavioral patterns, communication styles, attachment issues, traditions and habits (Sandwell, 2008). This does not mean that we who live in the present cannot heal from such wounds. Indeed, present generations can embrace God's grace toward healing, inner freedom and peace. In fact, living with such awareness of this potential for change is actually a blessing because of being trusted as the *transitional generation* that heals not only the present and past, but also heals any destructive physical, psycho-spiritual patterns that have the potential for wounding generations in the future. Remember, as we heal ourselves, we heal others, or as Franciscan priest Richard Rohr puts it: *transformed people, transform people* (Rohr, 2009).

Perhaps the most powerful example of God's grace at work in a generation is found in the genealogy of Jesus as recorded in Matthew 1:1-17.

> *This is the genealogy of Jesus the Messiah the son of David, the son of Abraham: Abraham was the father of Isaac, Isaac the father of Jacob, Jacob the father of Judah and his brothers, Judah the father of Perez and Zerah, whose mother was Tamar, Perez the father of Hezron, Hezron the father of Ram, Ram the father of Amminadab, Amminadab the father of Nahshon, Nahshon the father of Salmon, Salmon the father of Boaz, whose mother was Rahab, Boaz the father of Obed, whose mother was Ruth, Obed the father of Jesse, and Jesse the father of King David.*

David was the father of Solomon, whose mother had been Uriah's wife, Solomon the father of Rehoboam, Rehoboam the father of Abijah, Abijah the father of Asa, Asa the father of Jehoshaphat, Jehoshaphat the father of Jehoram, Jehoram the father of Uzziah, Uzziah the father of Jotham, Jotham the father of Ahaz, Ahaz the father of Hezekiah, Hezekiah the father of Manasseh, Manasseh the father of Amon, Amon the father of Josiah, and Josiah the father of Jeconiah and his brothers at the time of the exile to Babylon.

After the exile to Babylon: Jeconiah was the father of Shealtiel, Shealtiel the father of Zerubbabel, Zerubbabel the father of Abihud, Abihud the father of Eliakim, Eliakim the father of Azor, Azor the father of Zadok, Zadok the father of Akim, Akim the father of Elihud, Elihud the father of Eleazar, Eleazar the father of Matthan, Matthan the father of Jacob, and Jacob the father of Joseph, the husband of Mary, and Mary was the mother of Jesus who is called the Messiah. Thus there were fourteen generations in all from Abraham to David, fourteen from David to the exile to Babylon, and fourteen from the exile to the Messiah.

Even if you are not a regular reader of the Bible, there are some names you might recognize here. However, not so easy to spot are the scandals that existed in biblical times. In fact, we might go so far as to consider this list as Matthew's "R-Rated version" of sordid tales of murder, incest, rape, thievery, lying, stealing, cheating and lusting. In other words, the truth that lurks in the shadows. For example, let us read this genealogy again and consider the following:

- Tamar and Judah: Judah committed incest with his daughter in law in Genesis 38.
- Rahab was a prostitute and idol worshipper from Jericho whose life was spared after she hid the Israelite spies in Joshua 2:1-22.
- Ruth was originally a Moabite. Moabites were the race of people that resulted from incest between Lot and his oldest daughter (Genesis 19:30-36). As a result, the Moabites were forbidden by God from entering into the assembly of the Lord to the tenth generation (Deuteronomy 23:3). In spite of this judgment, the Israelites were commanded by God not to annihilate them, and were forbidden to marry them. However, Boaz marries Ruth and they have a son, Obed, who fathered a son named Jesse, who was the father of David, who became king of Israel.
- David committed adultery with another man's wife (Bathsheba), then had her husband killed (Uriah) in battle (2 Samuel 11). The child born out of wedlock eventually died. Later, David and Bathsheba had another son named Solomon, who became the heir to the throne of David.
- Within David's family there was strife between his other children: Absalom, Annon and Tamar. Tamar was

raped by her brother Annon, who is eventually killed by his brother Absalom (2 Samuel 13).

- Ahaz King of Judah raised pagan worship places and sacrificed his son to a pagan god.

- Hezekiah (Ahaz's other son) King of Judah brought sweeping reform to Israel, but then. . .

- Manasseh (Hezekiah's son) King of Judah built temples to pagan gods, approved of astrology and witchcraft and child sacrifice.

- And, by all outward appearances, Joseph believed Mary was unfaithful to him because she was pregnant before their marriage (Matthew 1:18-21). As a result, he wanted to divorce her quietly but later was told by God that her pregnancy did not result from a physical union.

All down through these 42 generations there seemed to be one public scandal after another. Yet, despite these so-called *rotten apples on the family tree* of Jesus, God's grace still provided for Jesus to redeem humanity from its sin and brokenness. For our lives today, I like to believe that not only did Matthew included this genealogy to fulfill one of the 44 prophecies that Jesus came from the Messianic line promised to David (2 Samuel 7:12-13, Isaiah 9:7), but also to demonstrate that in spite of human circumstances, nobody is beyond the grace of God. Nobody is beyond the redemptive power of God's love to bring about authenticity. This awareness alone ought to give us tremendous hope, as well as empower us to realize that we are not irreversibly bound to ancestral trauma or pain. On the contrary, God's grace and healing are available to all who seek transformation and transcendence for the betterment of themselves and for the entire world.

Something Greater Than Ourselves

Despite our perceived differences in race, language, religion and culture, there is a common Native American expression that emphasizes interconnectedness among all that we see, namely *Mitakuye Oyasin* (All Are Related). This phrase is understood by the Lakota Sioux people as an expression extending to all of Creation. Everything, i.e., humanity, animals, vegetation, minerals, elements, land, water, thunder, fire, wind, sun, moon, stars, etc., are connected to one another and affects one another. For too long, humanity has been influenced by the *"what's in it for me?"* scenarios. And as much as we can become enthralled by our gifts and giftedness, we must remember that our talents, skills, blessings, knowledge and wisdom are not for ourselves. These gifts are for the benefit of someone else. Reclaiming our authenticity compels us to now ask *how can we serve humanity? How can we alleviate suffering? How can we speak up for those who do not have a voice?* This is what authenticity is realty all about. Some might say that they are content being who they are. But we need to ask ourselves, *"Am I being authentic today?" Am I being honest and genuine in my relationships?* Why are we waiting till we are retired (whenever that will be) to do what we have always dreamed of doing? What are we waiting for? Having all our bills paid? Having enough money in the bank?

Too many people play the *I'll get around to it someday* game, while vulnerable and wounded people are in need now.

Such hurting people need others to see in them the potential to live authentically, including the benefit of reclaiming authenticity. Perhaps people believe they have too much to lose to be authentic? Perhaps they do not know or fear that people will not accept them as they are. Perhaps they have a fear of rejection, ridicule, shamed, ostracized, or shunned. The Native Americans have a saying passed down from ancient times: *The strength of a tree comes not from growing thicker in the good years when there is water, but from staying alive in the bad, dry times.* We live in a time when, as we focus on the virtue of stewardship, the one gift that we need to foster and treasure is the gift of our self, our inner life, our spirit of resiliency. There is great value in reclaiming our authenticity because we find an inner freedom and strength, peace and assurance of who we are without giving away our uniqueness playing by someone else's rules, definitions and expectations. For some, finding their inner strength to stand on their own two feet further empowers them to reach out for better relationships, jobs and justice. Indeed, those who are authentic often find God's blessing. I believe this is where the next great spiritual awakening will come from: Finding the strength to reclaim our authenticity.

A common expression that cuts across all generations, races and cultures is that we reap what we sow (Galatians 6:7-9). Many agricultural societies understand this concept better than others who have never put a seed in the ground. If you have good soil, good seed, enough water, sun and care, a healthy crop will be produced. The Chinese have a saying that *"if a man plants melons he will reap melons; if he sows beans, he will reap beans."* In other words, every action will produce an outcome, consequence or reward. And yet, there is another way to express this same idea in terms of character:

> *One evening an old Cherokee told his grandson about a battle that goes on inside people. He said, "My son, the battle is between two "wolves" inside us all. One is Evil. It is anger, envy, jealousy, sorrow, regret, greed, arrogance, self-pity, guilt, resentment, inferiority, lies, false pride, superiority, and ego. The other is Good. It is joy, peace, love, hope, serenity, humility, kindness, benevolence, empathy, generosity, truth, compassion, and faith." The grandson thought about it for a minute and then asked his grandfather: "Which wolf wins?" The old Cherokee simply replied, "The one you feed."*
>
> An old Cherokee teaching

Certainly, that which we feed (physically, emotionally and spiritually), grows to produce more of the same. This concept is true whether we are referring to agriculture or our own human desires. Still another way to understand this reality of cause/effect is through the symbol of the Cornucopia, i.e., the time-honored symbol of abundance, long associated with Thanksgiving. Tiwa Native American, ceremonial dancer, shaman, writer and artist Joseph Rael (*Beautiful Painted Arrow*) speaks about a vision of the Horn of Plenty he had in 2006:

On April 16, 2006, I was doing a dance in Australia when the Horn of Plenty appeared above the dance ground. The fruits of the Horn of Plenty began to fall into the dance arbor. . .It is spilling out into a spiral, which means it is germinating whatever is being seeded there. . .Abundance is coming to all of us who are living on the Earth at this time and to our children, grandchildren, and great-grandchildren. . .What the vision means is that there has been a major shift here. From the germination of the seeds will come the flowering of change. We humans have fooled around long enough, and God is going to take over. From now on we are going to get plenty of everything we focus and act on. If we focus on conflict, we will get more conflict. However, if we focus on peace we will get plenty of peace. As soon as we focus on a goal, the universe will take us in that direction. . .It is important for the future generations that when we elders leave this world, we leave it a better place for our children, our grandchildren, our great-grandchildren. You are here on Earth at this time because you are supposed to be here as their fathers, mothers, grandparents, aunts and uncles. You will pass this peace on to future generations and your responsibility will become their responsibility.

Sound: Native Teachings and
Visionary Art, (2009)

We live in a time when this is truer than ever before. The choice is ours. What we going to feed? If we feed inauthenticity then we will simply get more of the same. If we feed genuineness we will get more of this. Once we understand this teaching, the blame game starts and stops with us. Are we going to be content to throw up our hands and fatalistically say: *"That's just the way the world is, nothing we can do about it."* Or, do we realize that one simple act of kindness, love and authenticity sends out ripples of transformation that will wash back ashore to us. We have been given tremendous power, too much power at times because without authenticity of the self, that power is dangerous as history has taught. On the other hand, with authenticity comes a correct use of power tempered with wisdom and grace for the betterment of all. Reclaiming our authenticity means we now have the capacity to change; *the power to be that which has yet to be realized.* When we experience psycho-spiritual transformation we catch a glimpse of the beginning of something greater than ourselves with the unlimited potential for life, especially when we dance!

> *Dance, then, wherever you may be, I am the Lord of the dance, said he, And I'll lead you all, wherever you may be, And I'll lead you all in the dance, said he.*
> The Lord of The Dance, Sydney Carter (1963)

REFERENCES

Adler, A. (2009). *What life could mean to you: The psychology of personal development.* Oneworld Publications.

Alighieri, Dante (2013). *Inferno: Benton Classics.* Durante Divina Publishing House.

Beck, J.R. (1999). *Jesus and personality theory: Exploring the five-factor model.* Intervarsity Press.

Bodo, M. (2007). *Mystics: Ten who show us the ways of God.* St. Anthony Messenger Press.

Brown, F, Driver, S.R., Briggs, C.A. (1979). *The new Brown-Driver-Briggs-Gensenius Hebrew and English lexicon: With an appendix containing biblical Aramaic.* Hendrikson.

Brown, J.E. (1953). *The sacred pipe: Black Elk's account of the seven rites of the Oglala Souix.* Norman, OK: University of Oklahoma Press.

Brown, R. and Moloney, F. (2003). *An introduction to the Gospel of John: The anchor Yale Bible reference library.* Yale University Press.

Byock, I. (2004). *The Four Things That Matter Most: A Book About Living.* Atria Books.

Collins, J.C. and Vickers, J.E. (2013). *The Sermons of John Wesley: A collection for the Christian journey.* Abingdon Press.

Cousins, E. (1978). *Bonaventure: The soul's journey into God, the tree of life, the life of St. Francis (The Classics of Western Spirituality).* Paulist Press.

Coyhis, D.L. (2007). *Meditations with Native American elders: The four seasons.* Colorado Springs, CO: Coyhis Publishing & Consulting, Inc.

Delio, I., O.S.F. (2009). *The humility of God: A Franciscan perspective.* St. Anthony Messenger Press.

Diagnostic and Statistical Manual of Mental Disorders, 5th edition. (2013). American Psychiatric Association.

Duran, E. and Duran, B. (1995). *Native American postcolonial psychology.* Albany, NY: State University of New York Press.

Eiseley, L.C. (1969). *The Star thrower: The unexpected universe.* Harcourt, Brace and World.

Erikson, E. and Erikson, J. (1998). *The life cycle completed (extended version).* W. W. Norton & Company.

Frankl, V. (1997). *Man's search for meaning.* Mass Market Paperback.

Greyson, B. (2000). Near-death experiences. In E. Cardena, S.J. Lynn, and S. Krippner (eds.), *Varieties of anomalous experiences* (pp. 315-352). American Psychiatric Association.

Hall, R., Moore, D., Vincent, L. (2006). *Same kind of different as me.* Thomas Nelson.

The Holy Bible: New International Version

Houdini, H. (2004). *A magician among the spirits*. Fredonia Books.

Jackson, T. *The sermons of John Wesley - 1872 edition*. Retrieved from http://wesley.nnu.edu/john-wesley/the-sermons-of-john-wesley-1872-edition/

James, W. (2013). *Varieties of religious experience*. CreateSpace Independent publishing Platform.

Janoff-Bulman, R. (2002). *Shattered assumptions: Towards a new psychology of trauma*. Free Press.

Jeffreys, J.S. (2011). *Helping people grieve: When tears are not enough, 2nd edition*. Routledge.

Keating, T. (2009). *Intimacy with God: An introduction to centering prayer*. Crossraod Publishing Company.

Kidder, T. (2003). *Mountains beyond mountains: The quest of Dr. Paul Farmer, a man who would cure the world*. Random House Trade.

Langer, E. (1997). The Power of Mindful Learning. Reading, Mass: Addison-Wesley, page 99-100. (1997).

Linn, M. (2009). *Imprint*. Mti Home Video.

London, P. (2003). *Drawing closer to nature: Making art in dialogue with the natural world.* Shambhala.

May, R. (1994). *The discovery of being: Writings in existential psychology*. W.W. Norton and Company.

McAlpin, K. (2009). *Ministry that transforms: A contemplative process of theological reflection:* Liturgical Press.

Medwick, C. (1999). *Teresa of Avila: The progress of a soul*. New York: Alfred A Knopf.

Mitchell, D. (2004). *Cloud atlas*. New York: Random House.

Merton, T. (2007). *New seeds of contemplation*: New Directions; reprint edition.

Moore, T. (1994). *Care of the soul: A guide for cultivating depth and sacredness in everyday life.* HarperPerennial; reprint edition.

Naquin, S. and Yu, C. (1992). *Pilgrims and sacred sites in China.* University of California Press.

Nouwen, H. (1994). *Return of the prodigal son.* Image Books/ Doubleday.

Peers, E.A. and Teresa of Avila (2007). *The interior castle:* Dover Publications.

Perls, F. (1969). *In and out the garbage pail.* Gestalt Journal Press.

Perls, F., Hefferline, R. and Goodman, P. (1977) *Gestalt therapy: Excitement and growth in the human personality.* Gestalt Journal Press.

Piaget, J. (1932). *The moral judgment of the child.* New York: Harcourt, Brace and World.

Piedmont, R. L. (1999). Does spirituality represent that sixth factor of personality? Spiritual transcendence and the five factor model. *Journal of Personality,* 67, 985- 1013.

Powell, Peter. (1998). *Sweet medicine: Continuing role of the sacred arrows, the sun dance, and the sacred buffalo hat in northern Cheyenne history* (Civilization of the American Indian Series, 2 Volume Set). University of Oklahoma Press.

Rael, J. and Marlow, M.E. (1993). *Being and vibration.* Millichap Books.

Rael, J. (2009). *Sound: Native teaching and visionary art.* Millichap Books.

Randolf, R. W. (1937). *Sweet medicine and other stories of the Cheyenne Indians.* The Caxton Printers, ltd.

Roberts, L. and Levy, R. (2008). *Shamanic reiki: Expanded ways of working with universal life force.* Winchester, United Kingdom: O Books.

Rogers, C. R. (1951). *Client-centered therapy: Its current practice, implications and theory.* London: Constable.

Rogers, C. R. (1985). The necessary and sufficient conditions of therapeutic personality change in the *Journal of Consulting Psychology,* 2:95-103.

Rogers, C. R. (1995). *On becoming a person*: Mariner Books.

Roberts, L. and Levy, R. (2008). *Shamanic Reiki: Expanded ways of working with universal life force energy.* Moon Books.

Rohr, Richard, OSF. (2009). *The naked now: Learning to see as the mystics see.* The Crossroad Publishing Company.

Ross, A.C. (2000). *Crazy Horse and the real reason for the battle of the Little Big Horn.* Wiconi Waste.

Ruiz, D.M. (1997). *The four agreements: A practical guide to personal freedom.* Amber-Allen Publishing.

Sandwell, P. G. (2008). *Solving people problems for the creation and preservation of family wealth.* Salt Pond Press.

Sardello, R., Schroeder-Sheker, T and Sanders-Sardello, C. (2009). *Silence: The mystery of wholeness.* North Atlantic Books.

Satir, V., Bandler, R, and Grinder, J. (1976). *Changing with families: A book about further education for being human.* Palo Alto, CA: Science and Behavior Books.

Satir, V. (1978). *Your many faces.* Berkley, CA: Celestial Arts.

Satir, V. (1983). *Conjoint therapy*: Palo Alto, CA: Science and Behavior Books.

Schaffer, R (1996). *Social Development.* Oxford: Blackwell.

Shuman, J. and Meador, K. (2003). *Heal thyself: Spirituality, medicine and the distortion of Christianity.* New York: Oxford University Press.

Stolzman, W. (1995). *The pipe and Christ: A Christian-Sioux dialogue.* Tipi Press.

Stoudt, E., Jacquin, L., and Atwater, P.M.H. (2006). *Six major challenges faced by near-death experiencers* in the Journal of Near-Death Studies, Vol 25, No. 1. Pp. 49-62.

Strong, J. (2010). The new Strong's expanded exhaustive concordance of the Bible. Thomas Nelson.

Sulmasy, D. (1997). *The healer's calling: A spirituality for physicians and other health care providers.* Paulist Press.

Sun Bear, Wabun and Weinstock, B. (1987). *The path of power.* New York: Simon and Schuster.

Sun Bear. (1989). Walking in the balance: The path to healthy, happy and harmonious living. Simon & Schuster.

Sweeny, T. J. (2009). *Adlerian counseling and psychotherapy: A practitioner's approach, fifth edition.* Routledge.

Vygotsky, L. S. (1978). *Mind in society: The development of higher psychological processes.* Cambridge, MA: Harvard University Press.

Wapp, E. Jr. (1984). The American Indian courting flute: Revitalization and change, Contemporary American Indian Issues Series, Number 5, *Sharing a Heritage:*

American Indian Arts, edited by Charlotte Heth and Michael Swarm, 49–60.

Wada, S. (2002). The Ox Herder: A Zen Parable Illustrated. Braziller Publications.

Weisel, l E. (2006). *Night*. Hill and Wang, revised edition.

Wicks, R. (1995). *Touching the holy: Ordinariness, self-esteem and friendship.* Notre Dame, IN: Ave Maria Press.

Wigram, G.V. (1979). *The englishman's Greek concordance of the new testament.* Baker Book House Company.